A Beginner's Guide to

INVESTING IN NO-LOAD MUTUAL FUNDS

A Beginner's Guide to

❖

INVESTING IN NO-LOAD MUTUAL FUNDS

J. STANLEY LEVITT

❖

International Publishing Corporation, Inc.
Chicago, Illinois

ISBN# 0-942541-46-9

Library of Congress Catalog Card Number: 92-75856

First Edition

Published by International Publishing Corporation

This publication is designed to provide accurate and authoritative information in regard to the subject matter covered. It is sold with the understanding that the publisher is not engaged in rendering legal, accounting, or other professional service. If legal advice or other expert assistance is required, the services of a competent professional person should be sought.

Dedicated to my beloved wife
HARRIET
for 52 years of
unwavering
devotion

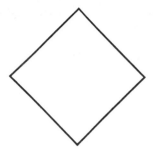

Table of Contents

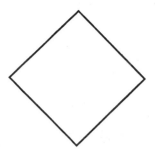

Prologue

I first become acquainted with no-load mutual funds in 1964. My mother's physician advised me that my mother was developing arteriosclerosis and recommended that I begin to take over her affairs. He indicated that she eventually would require nursing home care. In retrospect, her condition, I now believe, was Alzheimer's. My challenge then was how to make her funds, $52,000, stretch out for an unknown length of time to provide the best possible care.

My first step was to research the quality of care and the cost of available nursing homes. I found the finest nursing home with all the requisites, and the cost was $275 per month. I liquidated my mother's holdings in such stocks as Standard Oil and Kansas City Power & Light, invested $50,000 in a highly recommended no-load growth fund, requesting a systematic withdrawal check of $275 per month, and retained $2,000 in a local checking account for emergency purposes.

Mother lived two and a half years after entering the nursing home. When she passed away, the fund had remitted the monthly checks as requested, totaling $8,250 for the period, and was worth $58,000, a total return of 32.5 percent for the period, including the payout, or 13 percent per year. Obviously, without the payout the total return would have been considerably greater.

In the 1980s, having sold a successful business, I enrolled in adult study courses at Baruch College in New York, taking courses in finance, investments, and financial planning, as I had taken courses previously at UMKC and Kansas City Junior College in business law, economics, bookkeeping, accounting, and other related fields.

In 1985, I joined the American Association of Individual Investors (AAII), a nonprofit corporation formed for the purpose of assisting individuals in becoming effective managers of their own assets through programs of education, information, and research. In 1986, I returned to our native Kansas City where I learned a new local AAII chapter had been formed, and I volunteered to handle programming, subsequently becoming president of the chapter. I was able to bring to Kansas City individuals well-informed in various subjects of investment, and I feel indebted to them with whom I spent considerable time for adding immeasurably to my knowledge of investing, especially in no-load mutual funds. In alphabetical sequence: Mr. James Benham, Mr. Bill Donoghue, Mr. Al Frank, Mr. Don Gould, Mr. Joseph Granville, Mr. Mark Hulbert, Mr. Sheldon Jacobs, Mr. Paul Merriman, Mr. H. Bradlee Perry, Mr. Jay Schabacker, and Mr. Gordon Snyder. I was privileged to spend a full two days with most of them, and I sincerely thank each one for the discussions we held, as well as their talks to our AAII chapter.

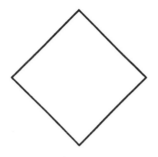

Introduction

There are many fine books on mutual funds written by knowledgeable authors. Most of these books are hardbound, containing upwards of 300 pages with numerous graphs and charts, as well as names and examples of the performance of various mutual funds at different periods in the history of the growth of the mutual fund industry.

All of these books are of benefit to the investor who has some knowledge and experience, and you are encouraged, after reading this book, to look into others to enhance your knowledge.

This book, *A Beginner's Guide to Investing in No-Load Mutual Funds,* is completely generic. It does not mention the name of any fund or fund family. The purpose is to teach the basics of mutual fund investing to you with little or no knowledge of the subject and to gradually increase your knowledge as you progress through this book until you have a complete understanding, including the sophisticated strategies of investing explained later in this book.

Therefore, the number of pages in this book has been kept to a minimum to get as directly as possible to the point of each subject. The more sophisticated investor may find a review of the basics beneficial and possibly learn something new in the strategies of investing.

Explaining The Mutual Fund Company

Mutual fund companies gather from investors money with which they purchase securities of many types—stocks, bonds, and money market instruments—for the benefit of you, the shareholder.

When you invest in a mutual fund you will buy a number of shares of the fund at the price the fund is worth on the day you make your purchase. This price is called the *net asset value*, and it is determined by dividing the total assets in the fund by the total number of shares owned by all of its investors. For example, if the fund has $30 million in assets and shareholders hold 2 million shares, then each share is worth $15 ($30 million divided by 2 million). That $15 is the *net asset value*, also referred to as the *NAV*. This price will fluctuate and is calculated daily. The closing NAV each day is based on: the closing market value of securities in the fund, the number of new shares purchased during the day, and the number of shares redeemed during the day.

TYPES OF INVESTMENT COMPANIES

The most popular fund is called an *open-end* fund. This means the mutual fund company issues new shares whenever it gets new investors or if the present investors invest more money in the fund. You will be able to sell your shares back to the mutual fund company directly at any time and receive the net asset value of the day for your shares.

Another type of investment company is called the closed-end fund. We're going to take another minute or two to explain about *closed-end* funds, but we will not deal with them in this book. Closed-end funds do not issue more shares. They are like a corporation in that respect, and you cannot sell your shares back to the closed-end fund company. These must be sold on the open stock market just like individual stocks or bonds. Consequently, they rarely sell at *NAV*, but usually at either a discount or a premium.

In this book we will deal with *open-end* funds. As an investor you will share in the fund's income, its expenses, and its profits and losses.

NO-LOAD MUTUAL FUNDS

In the title of this book you saw the words *no-load funds*. In the terminology of mutual funds, the word *load* means a commission and when we say *no-load*, it means there are no commissions. You do not have to buy no-load funds from a broker or salesperson. You will learn later in this book how to buy no-load funds directly from the no-load mutual fund company.

Paying a load (or commission) to a broker or salesperson does not mean getting a better fund, nor is it an inducement or incentive to the fund management to perform better. On the contrary, it may reduce the return on your investment as will be pointed out later in this chapter.

There are other types of charges besides commissions, and these—low-loads, 12b-1, and redemption fees—will be described later in this chapter.

ADVANTAGES OF NO-LOAD
MUTUAL FUND INVESTING

There are two important precautions before investing in anything: *Never invest in anything you don't understand* and *investigate before investing.* When you have finished reading this book you will thoroughly understand how to identify no-load funds, how to select the right funds for your particular age, family status, life-style, and financial objectives.

To understand no-load mutual funds, let's take a look at the advantages these mutual funds have to offer. These include diversification, low transaction costs, professional management, and safety.

Diversification

Investing in no-load mutual funds makes good sense. It does not prevent you from investing in individual stocks and bonds. However, if done properly, investing in the latter requires much more time for research and analysis. Let's assume that you spend one hour per day in such analysis; that amounts to one eighth of your earned income. Multiply five hours of earned income times 52 weeks and then compare that with the average mutual fund management fee of one-half of one percent of its assets per year; the management fee amounts to about $50 per $10,000 invested.

Yes, investing in no-load mutual funds requires some homework also, because diversification is very important. You can develop much more diversification with three or four mutual funds than owning only three or four stocks or bonds. You have the risk that the market may go down, and owning only three or four stocks or bonds could have a serious effect on your holdings. A mutual fund spreads that risk over a large number of securities in different industries that are unlikely to be affected in the same way at the same time.

Low Transaction Costs

When you have selected a mutual fund of interest (discussed in Chapter 5), you call their toll-free 800 number and request a prospectus. This prospectus gives complete information about the fund, its history, its earnings, its transaction costs, and will also include any unfavorable facts. We will discuss in detail how to read a prospectus in Chapter 6.

The no-load mutual fund's transaction costs are low. True, the fund pays commissions to purchase the securities it wants for its portfolio of stock, bonds, or money market instruments. However, because of its huge buying power these commissions or transactions costs are much lower—perhaps as low as five cents per share—than the same costs would be to the individual investor.

Professional Management of Your Investment

With no-load mutual funds, you will get experienced management, regular reports, and special services. The fund's past performance record is readily available for analysis and comparison with other similar funds. Though past performance is no guarantee of future results, comparing several funds of the same type with the same objectives, over a five- to ten-year period, will give you good indication of performance. Usually funds with good historical results will have the best management and the best chances of future results. As mentioned previously, you also get diversification through the fund's portfolio, thus reducing your risk considerably.

You will receive regularly, either monthly or quarterly, a statement showing your transactions and the value of your investment on the date of the statement, which makes tax reporting very simple.

The fund may also offer several special services, such as *automatic reinvestment* of your interest or dividends, which will rapidly compound the growth of your principal. There are systematic *withdrawal plans* available in which the fund will mail you a check once each month for the amount of money you select. You can arrange *telephone switch* privileges, wherein a phone call from you will result in your switching your investment to another fund in the same company.

You can arrange with the company to wire your funds in whole or in part to your bank account with just a phone call. You'll have those funds at your bank within 24 hours. That's real liquidity. Money market mutual funds and many bond funds will provide you with a *checkbook* to draw on your investment.

Most funds have a minimum investment, usually $1,000 or more, but a few have little or no minimum, and nearly all funds have a very low minimum for IRA or Keogh accounts.

When you invest in a fund you will be credited with the number of shares according to the closing price of the shares on the day your money is received by the fund. As stated before, this price is called the *net asset value* or *NAV*. By the same token, if you wish to redeem shares, which you may do by phone with most mutual fund companies (some require a letter), the redemption will be made at the NAV at 4 p.m. Eastern time the day you call or the day your letter is received.

WHY ARE MUTUAL FUNDS A SAFE INVESTMENT?

Since the inception of mutual funds in the 1920s, no fund has ever declared bankruptcy. As a rule, a fund that does poorly for an extended period of time will be merged into a more successful fund by the fund company or fund family. At which point, when the merger is completed, you will receive shares of equal value.

Theft from a mutual fund is virtually impossible since the securities are held by a third party, normally a bank or trust company called the transfer agent. Securities and Exchange Commission (SEC) regulation of mutual funds is much more stringent than it is for the general stock market. The value of your mutual fund shares can go up and down with the market but, unless you sell at a bad time, it is very unlikely that you will lose with a long-term investment in mutual funds.

THE MUTUAL FUND COMPANY OPERATION

We will explain here the format or structure of most mutual fund companies. There are, of course, bound to be some variations from one company to another. We will also discuss extra fees and charges established by some fund companies which can increase your cost of investing.

Usually the management company is the organization which formed the fund. There are individual mutual funds and *families* of mutual funds having a number of diversified funds. These families of funds in most cases started with only one fund. When you invest in a mutual fund you become a shareholder.

When the fund is originally organized, the owner or owners who invest in the company elect the officers and directors since they are the original shareholders. The board of directors, as in any corporation, is elected by the shareholders.

All mutual fund companies have an investment adviser responsible for the day-to-day management of the fund or funds. The board of directors will delegate this responsibility to the adviser who may be the officer of officers of the company or to an outside professional management firm.

The fund adviser receives a fee based on the fund's assets. The adviser hires skilled, professional individuals to be managers of the fund portfolios, purchasing stocks or bonds or short-term instruments for money market funds, depending on the type of fund or funds the adviser has delegated to the professional manager.

The adviser will employ a number of research analysts to monitor and analyze the financial condition of companies whose stocks are of interest. They will factor in general economic conditions, the trend of the market, and other data. Based on the information received from the analyst, the portfolio manager will make purchase decisions and usually maintain a portfolio of 60 to 100 different securities. This enormous holding in the portfolio greatly spreads and reduces the risk of loss way beyond the financial ability of the individual investor holding only a few stocks or bonds.

No-load funds will also have a custodian, usually, but not limited to, a bank, which safeguards the assets of the fund, making the payment for securities with the authority of the adviser. It also receives the funds you send to purchase your shares. Additionally, the fund adviser appoints a transfer agent who handles the recordkeeping requirements, issuing new shares when purchased by investors, cancels redeemed shares when an investor sells, and records dividend or interest payments.

The annual or semi-annual report, sent to shareholders automatically, provides information on where the fund has made its investments. This same information is also included in Part B of the prospectus, called the Statement of Additional Information. This statement should be requested when asking for a prospectus since it is not automatically included.

THE COSTS OF INVESTING IN MUTUAL FUNDS

There are a number of fees to be examined in all mutual funds, both load and no-load. Let's analyze these in order to keep your cost of investing to a minimum.

Adviser Fees

All mutual funds have adviser fees, and no-load funds average approximately one-half of one percent of the assets of the funds being managed.

Expense Ratio

All mutual funds have daily expenses like any other corporation. As a rule the total of adviser fees and expense ratio in no-load mutual stock funds will average approximately 1 percent to 1.2 percent, per year. No-load bond fund fees will average about half as much, approximately 0.50 basis points while load funds will average 0.75 to 0.80 basis points. As a rule, funds with lower assets will have a higher cost. However, many fund companies will have higher costs due to less efficient management. As a rule, based on review of monthly data covering over 2,600 mutual funds of all types, load funds will average higher costs than no-load funds.

Load or Commission

The front-end load is a fee taken right from the top of your investment in load funds. This commission ranges from 4.5 percent to 8.5 percent in load funds. A high commission does not mean you get a better fund or better performance. Just one more good reason to stick with no-load funds. A few funds, originally true no-load funds, have added a "low-load" of 2 percent and sometimes 3 percent .

12b-1 Fees

Up to 1.25 percent annually of the total fund assets may be taken by the management company to pay for advertising and publicity. This fee should be avoided although a few funds with outstanding records may charge a 12b-1 fee of 25 basis points (1/4 of one percent). This is not too objectionable in stock (equity) funds but it is in bond funds where the 12b-1 can have a greater long-term negative effect.

Redemption Fees

This fee is charged by some funds when shares are redeemed. Its purpose is to discourage redemptions. This fee can range upward from 1 percent.

Contingent Deferred Sales Charge (CDSC)

Instead of a front-end load, this CDSC (Contingent Deferred Sales Charge) expense is contingent upon the year shares are sold. The charge may be as much as 7 percent when you sell shares the first year declining by 1 percent per year thereafter so that you are encouraged to stay with the fund for 7 years. There are many more load funds than no-loads which charge this fee.

In Chapter 2, Figure 2-1 shows you a portion of a column from a typical mutual fund page appearing in most metropolitan newspapers. The fees described above, except adviser and expense fees, are all shown there. Explanations on how to recognize such fees and interpret the quotation symbols are included.

Stocks, Bonds, Load Mutual Funds vs. No-Load Funds

There are always a few investors who search for the "big killing" in a specific stock. Once in a while a stock does accomplish huge gains, and those individuals who happen to be investors at the time will, undoubtedly, let you know how much expertise they had in selecting that particular stock. However, most of the time, it is sheer luck. Such situations, of course, lend credence to the myth that the way to riches is to find that special stock which will double, triple, or even quadruple in price.

BUYING INDIVIDUAL STOCKS OR BONDS

If you feel that you have that uncanny knack, a superior knowledge, and you are willing to spend countless hours of spare time finding that "super stock," then go for it. However, there are few investors, including the professionals of Wall Street, who can fill that mold. It's the old fable of the tortoise and the hare. Most people who accumulate wealth do so through hard work, and steady, consistent saving and investing.

Selecting a good bull market year like 1985, the facts show us that the NYSE index was up 26.1 percent. Only 79 percent of the listed stocks had a gain. Only 18 percent gained 50 percent or more. So doubling or tripling your investment is, at best, a long shot and carries with it a high degree of volatility and risk. Additionally, brokerage fees can be very expensive while searching for the "big one".

More to the point, research has shown that, at any given time, stocks are priced where they ought to be, considering all the information available about them. When any new information is randomly developed about a stock that will influence its price, the average investor seldom knows about it until he reads the financial page the next day, after action has been taken on the stock by those few who were "in the know" early.

Stocks are not ordinarily overvalued or undervalued. Most professionals and most individual investors follow a limited number of stocks and buy or sell quickly when they feel a certain stock price is out of line.

Obtaining information about stocks and bonds is relatively easy; interpreting it *correctly* is much more difficult. As mentioned in Chapter 1, the cost of your time relative to your income is considerably higher than the management fee of a good no-load mutual fund.

Let's make a few comparisons. Let's say you want to own health-care stocks. There are several hundred health-care companies, but you can't possibly determine for yourself the very few which will still be doing business five years or ten years from now. Imagine merely finding out the basics about all the hospitals, nursing home chains, pharmaceutical manufacturers, manufacturers of health-care equipment, etc. Plus, you should also know the quality of these companies, the management, its history, and its future prospects.

There are a number of mutual funds which specialize in portfolios of health-care stocks. A health-care mutual fund has the contacts, the resources, and the information to know which are the top producing companies to include in its portfolio. You can purchase shares in the best performing no-load health-care mutual funds, if that's your interest, and leave your investment to be managed by the professionals.

Do you prefer municipal bonds? How many individual bonds of this type can you afford to own? If one or two default, that would probably have a strong impact on your portfolio. In a municipal bond mutual fund a default of a single bond would hardly be noticeable among such a large portfolio of diversified bonds.

In my opinion, the no-load mutual fund is an ideal investment for the average person who wants to accumulate wealth gradually over a period of time with the greatest amount of safety and diversification. In just ten years mutual funds have grown from 130 billion dollars to one trillion dollars in assets. That should be evidence enough that more and more investors are finding mutual funds the most suitable investment available.

SAFETY VERSUS SOME RISK

Many people say to me, "I want my money to be absolutely safe." I have no criticism, so let's take a look at the safest choices—U.S. Treasury bills, notes and bonds, and Certificates of Deposit (CDs). In Chapters 3 and 4, we'll look at some mutual funds whose objective is to contain a percentage of these *safe investments* in their portfolio.

U.S. Treasury Bills, Notes and Bonds

Most individuals who invest in treasuries do so because they know they will always get their money back and, if they hold these instruments until maturity, they will get their initial investment both with interest but no growth.

The cost and maturities of bills, notes, and bonds vary as follows:

- Treasury *bills* can be purchased in $10,000 amounts only and mature in one year or less.

- Treasury *notes* are available in denominations of $1,000 and $5,000. Maturities range from one to ten years.

- Treasury *bonds* can be purchased in amounts of $1,000 and have maturities of ten to thirty years.

The effect of inflation and taxes on the interest can be devastating when you own individual instruments, however. And there are other disadvantages to owning individual or a limited amount of treasuries: Selling them before the maturity dates could cause you to lose part of your investment. Purchasing in the larger dollar amounts, as indicated above, results in limiting the number of treasuries you can own. Consequently, if interest rates increase, the value of your treasuries, like other bonds, goes down; of course, they will increase in value if interest rates decrease.

On the other hand, you can own hundreds of treasuries by investing in no-load mutual funds specializing in this area. There are short-, intermediate-, and long-term treasury and government bond funds. Fund managers are constantly buying and selling to keep their fund portfolio current, thereby limiting the effect of inflation. Additionally, treasury mutual funds can grow so that your total return can, in periods of downward movement of interest rates, can be equal in growth to some stock funds. By contrast, when interest rates rise, the value of the bond and the bond fund will go down. But once again, in the fund you have the cushion of safety in numbers and diversification. More about fixed-income funds later in Chapter 4.

The Safety of Certificates of Deposit (CDs)

These investments, when issued by federally insured savings and loans, banks, or credit unions, are quite safe from loss of principal up to $100,000 for each account on your name alone; another $100,000 per account is insured in your spouse's name. However, early withdrawal penalties can be as much as three months' interest.

The Advantage of No-Load Funds

Since you would be penalized for early sale of your treasuries or early cashing of your CDs, plus the fact that inflation and taxes can reduce your gains to practically nothing, does it not make good sense to invest in no-load mutual funds? Funds which offer a high degree of safety with long-term investments which will earn considerably more, offsetting the erosion of inflation and taxes?

With a few hundred dollars you can have ownership of many treasury bills and bonds in a no-load mutual fund and still have the full faith and credit of the U.S. Government. You also can redeem your money on a daily basis and not wait for maturity dates of individual bills or bonds nor have to sell them in a secondary market.

Additional investments such as buying stocks, bonds, unit investment trusts, "Ginnie Mae" certificates, and load funds carry a high cost, making no-load mutual funds all the more attractive. The costs of other investments are shown in Table 2-1 on page 16.

HOW TO IDENTIFY MUTUAL FUNDS FROM THE FINANCIAL PAGE

In Figure 2-1 on page 17 we have taken a part of a financial page and explained the various symbols which

TABLE 2-1: COMMISSIONS ON A $100,000 INVESTMENT

Type of Investment	*Commission Range*
No-Load Mutual Fund	Zero
Treasury Securities (*Purchased direct*)	$50.00
Municipal Bonds	$1,000 - $2,000
Unit Investment Trust	$3,000 - $4,900
Common Stocks	$1,000 - $3,000
Load Mutual Fund	$1,000 - $9,300
New Stock Offering	$3,000 - $10,000
Limited Partnership	$6,000 - $10,000

will help you identify no-load mutual funds and those with extra charges other than management fees. This format is common with most metropolitan papers. Information comes by retrieval from Dow Jones. As an example, let's look at three of the funds from Figure 2-1 referenced with an arrow.

Fund	NAV	Offer Price	NAV Change
GISI r	9.41	9.41	-.01
HiYld p	6.84	NL	+.01
Sellnc p	6.52	NL	......

The first fund indicated, GISI, tells us that the fund closed with a net asset value of $9.41, the offer price indicates that this is a load fund whose NAV decreased by -.01 from the previous close. The second fund, HiYld, a no-load fund with a 12b-1 plan, shows an increase in NAV of +.01 from the previous day. The third fund, Sellnc p, also a no-load fund with a 12b-1 plan, indicates that there was no change in NAV.

FIGURE 2-1: MUTUAL FUNDS QUOTATIONS

Columbia Funds			
Balance	16.38	NL +	.06
ComStk	13.50	NL +	.11
Fixed	13.59	NL −	.05
Govt	8.55	NL −	.02
Grth	27.20	NL +	.10
Muni	12.09	NL	......
Specl	17.46	NL +	.13
Fortress Invst			
AdiRt †	9.93	9.93	......
Bond r	9.23	9.23	......
→ GISI r	9.41	9.41	.01
MunIn †	10.54	10.65	......
Util r	12.02	12.14 +	.02
44Wall	2.28	2.28 +	.01
TxEx p	11.54	12.12 −	.01
Wsh p x	16.39	17.39 +	.10
A GthFd	8.60	9.40 +	.08
A Heritg	1.12	NL +	.01
A Invst	5.52	5.78 −	.05
A Inv In	5.36	5.61 −	.24
Amer Natl Funds			
Grth	4.80	5.12 +	.02
Inco	22.76	24.28 +	.16
Triflex	16.01	17.08 +	.04
API Gr fp	10.80	10.80 −	.02
Am Perform			
Bond	10.84	11.29 −	.03
Equity	11.67	12.16 +	.08
IntBd	10.76	11.09 −	.03
AmUtlFd	21.87	21.87 +	.08
Amway f	7.67	7.91 +	.08
Analyt	12.58	NL +	.08
Financial Invesco			
→ HiYld p	6.84	NL +	.01
→ SelInc p	6.52	NL	......
USGvt p	7.45	NL −	.03
Dynm p	10.29	NL +	.03
Emgrth p	8.61	NL +	.03
Indust p	4.90	NL +	.04
IndInc p	10.71	NL +	.03
Eqty	16.45	NL +	.17
Flex	17.06	NL +	.12
IntGov	12.79	NL −	.05
IntlGr	12.29	NL −	.08
Leisur	16.34	NL +	.05
FinSvc	15.30	NL +	.02
PcBas	11.05	NL +	.03
HlthSc	35.60	NL −	.05
Envirn	7.57	NL +	.03
Tech	20.26	NL +	.06
Enrgy	9.17	NL +	.03
Europ	10.05	NL −	.09

The first column is the fund's name, often abbreviated. Several funds listed under a single heading indicate a family of funds. Letters following the fund name are explained below.

A "t" indicates the fund has both a "p" and an "r" (are listed below).

An "r" after the name indicates the fund has either a redemption fee or a CDSC (a contingent deferred sales charge). Applied when shares are sold.

"p" means the fund has a 12b-1 plan.

"x" indicates the fund went ex-dividend the previous day. (See glossary.)

An "f" indicates the price is for the previous day.

"e" is "ex", a capital gains distribution. (See glossary).

"s" the fund split its shares or declared a stock dividend.

The second column is the net asset value (NAV) per share as of the close of the preceding business day. In some newspapers, the NAV is identified as the sell or the bid price—the amount, per share, you would receive if you sold your shares, less any deferred sales charges.

The third column is the offering price or, in some papers, the buy or asked price—the price you would pay if you purchased shares. The buy price is the NAV plus any sales charges. NL for no-load, appears in this column, and the buy price is the same as the NAV, the second column. If the NAV and the offer price are the same, it means the fund has no initial load, but it does have a CDSC.

The fourth column shows the change, if any, in NAV from the preceding quotation—in other words, the change over the most recent one-day trading period.

THE SALES PITCH FOR LOAD FUNDS

In the wake of the success of no-load funds and a more informed investor, brokers and brokerage houses are attempting to sell load funds by making the following statements (Note: The actual facts follow the statements):

1. The no-load benefit is for the short-term investor. *Fact:* It's beneficial for the long-term investor.

2. Admittedly, load funds charge more for the first few years, but the condition could reverse itself with the on-going management fees in no-load funds. *Fact:* Load funds also have on-going management fees.

3. No-loads are not no-loads. They collect fees over longer periods of time. *Fact:* Not true. Load funds collect fees annually and many more load funds have 12b-1, redemption, and CDSC fees than no-loads.

These statements imply that no-loads have higher expense ratios than load funds and that they are, in the long run, more expensive than load funds since most load funds charge only the initial sales fee. In fact, no-load funds do *not* have a higher, on average, expense ratio than load funds. A recent fee table comparing 500 load-fund expenses with no-load fund expenses over a ten-year period found only seven of the load funds were in the top 300 of all funds with the lowest cost. The other 293 were all *no-load* funds.

And, an even more recent study conducted by Morningstar, Inc., a leading fund research service, and reported by the *No-Load Fund X* in August 1992, found that pure no-load funds (those without front-end or back-end loads, 12b-1 fees, or ongoing redemption fees, enjoyed lower average expense ratios in both small and large funds. Further findings showed that load charges, in fact, do little to increase fund size. This is contrary to the load fund sales pitch that loads generate larger funds, which in turn produce lower expenses, which in turn benefit load fund investors. And no- loads overall have higher expense ratios there are no free lunches.

Not true. No-loads simply cost less to purchase and sell, and, on average, cost less to hold. And they have an edge in performance. This Morningstar study was made for the 100% No-Load Mutual Fund Council, a trade association of No-Load funds.

No-Load Fund X newsletter studies have always found that the presence or absence of loads has nothing to do with actual investment performance. Loads just cost you money. The foregoing study carries the no-load advantages beyond just savings, with the advantage of lower on-going expense ratios.

Again, as a no-load fund investor you have your choice of approximately 1,300 no-load funds without the pressure of a salesperson trying sell you a fund you don't know anything about.

LOAD FUNDS VERSUS NO-LOAD FUNDS

Why are no-load funds better than load funds? Because you do not need a broker to help you decide on 1 or more funds. Following is why.

A broker has a different objective than you do. Your interest is long-term investing. A broker makes money (a commission) only when he makes a sale or redemption. A broker can sell you only the funds offered by his brokerage house, limiting your selection, and those funds may not have a good track record or may not be the type of fund you need for your circumstances.

No-load funds are every bit as good as load funds, so why pay for something you don't need? *Example*: If you were to invest $10,000 each in 1 load fund and 1 no-load fund and your load (commission) amounted to 8.5 percent, you are starting your load fund with only $9,150, but your no-load fund invests the full $10,000. If both funds perform identically over the next 10 years, your no-load fund will be worth $2,204 more than the load fund, presuming the growth has been an even 10 percent per year.

At the end of the first year, your load fund will be worth, at 10 percent, only $10,065. Your no-load fund will be worth $11,000. The longer you keep your two investments, the wider the difference becomes, all because of the original load.

Even investing equal amounts in two different no-load funds, 1 of which has a 1 percent 12b-1 fee, with both funds growing at the rate of 10 percent per year and the initial investment in each fund of $10,000, the pure no-load will be worth $2,263 more than the fund with the 12b-1, which is an annual expense fee. The 1 percent reduces the growth of the second fund to 9 percent per year as opposed to the 10 percent growth of the true no-load. (See Figures 2-2 and 2-3.)

From these illustrations you can see that any kind of load will affect the long-term performance, whether it is a low-load of 3 or 2 percent, a 12b-1, or a redemption fee (sometimes called a contingent deferred sales charge (CDSC).

Additionally, you should disregard expense ratios which can run from a low of 0.25 basis points to as high as 2 percent. If your funds are doing a much better job of growth in comparison with other funds having the same objectives, you really do not care about these low expense ratios. However, keep in mind that adding commissions (or loads) to the expense ratios makes a whale of a difference in the end results.

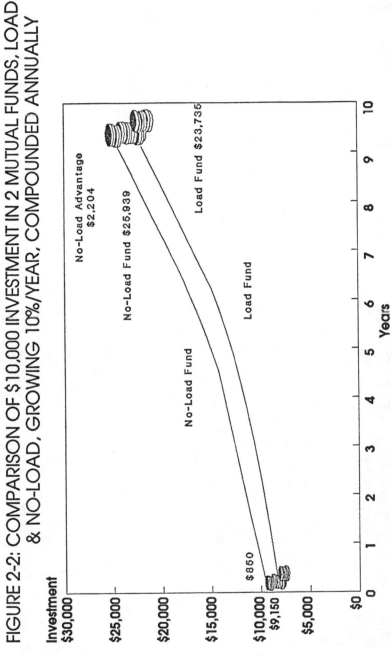

FIGURE 2-2: COMPARISON OF $10,000 INVESTMENT IN 2 MUTUAL FUNDS, LOAD & NO-LOAD, GROWING 10%/YEAR, COMPOUNDED ANNUALLY

FIGURE 2-3: COMPARISON OF TWO FUNDS WITH IDENTICAL PERFORMANCE EXCEPT ONE FUND HAS A 1% 12B-1 CHARGE

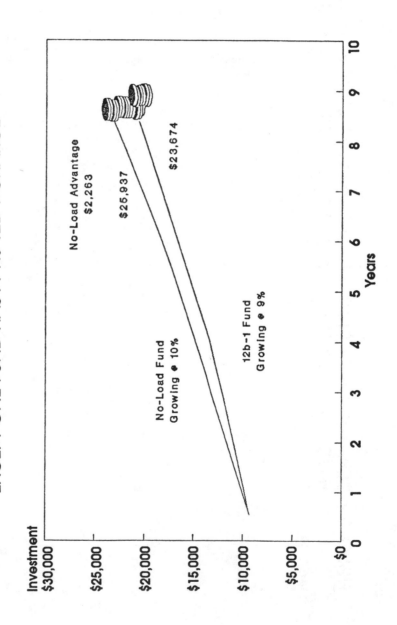

Equity and Money Market Mutual Funds

There are six *basic* types of mutual funds. There are numerous names of funds, but each of them falls in one of these broad categories:

> Aggressive Growth funds
> Growth funds
> Growth and Income funds
> Income funds
> Fixed Income funds
> Money Market funds

Each of the above types of funds have a different amount of volatility and therefore will have varied degrees of risk and reward. To determine how much volatility there is to each fund, we apply a beta rating. This is an indication of market risk of the fund's sensitivity to the movement of the stock market in general —usually the S&P 500 Index. Funds with the same movement as the market are regarded as having a beta of 1.00. Those having greater movement, or more volatility, will have a higher beta; those with less volatility, a lower beta. With this in mind, let us then proceed to describe each of the six basic funds. Table 3-1 provides a summary of fund characteristics. Pointers for selecting the right mutual fund categories for you will be discussed in Chapter 7.

TABLE 3-1: FUND CHARACTERISTICS

Fund Category	Investment Portfolio	Objective	Risk
Aggressive Growth	Stocks	Maximum Capital Gain	Highest
Growth	Stocks	Long Term Capital Gain	High
Growth & Income	Stocks, Bonds	Growth & Income	Moderate
Income	Stocks, Bonds	Income & Growth Potential	Moderate
Fixed Income	Bonds	High Income, Stability	Low
Money Market	T-bills, CDs, Commercial Paper	Liquidity, Preservation of Capital	Lowest

AGGRESSIVE GROWTH FUNDS

The objective of an aggressive growth fund is to obtain maximum capital gain without regard to income. The fund managers may invest in stocks of smaller capitalization which carry greater risk. They may "leverage" their portfolio, borrowing money to buy additional stocks. They may sell short, and they may write options.

Aggressive growth funds do well in bull markets but poorly in bear markets. They can be rewarding to long-term investors, those who hold the aggressive funds for five years or longer. They have a greater risk for short-term investors and for investors who have a low tolerance of volatility or risk. The average beta for aggressive growth funds in 1990 was 1.13. Other names for aggressive growth funds: performance funds, and the newer sector funds (funds investing in only one industry such as utilities, health, telecommunications), and common stock funds. Capital appreciation funds and maximum capital gains funds are also aggressive growth funds as are precious metals funds.

GROWTH FUNDS

A growth fund's objective is to increase the value of your investment with less risk than the aggressive growth funds assume. As a rule they do not use leverage or short selling, but invest in larger, more stable companies. Growth fund managers tend to build up more cash reserves during periods when the trend of the market is uncertain, thereby giving more conservative balance to their portfolio. The performance of growth funds will be more stable than aggressive growth and will perform more consistently.

Volatility of the average growth fund will be less than the market. We indicated in the description of aggressive growth funds that they were 13 percent more volatile than the market (beta 1.13). The average growth fund in 1990 was 12 percent less volatile than the market with an average beta of .88. If you want to see your money grow sufficiently to keep you ahead of inflation, but without the adventuresome risks of the aggressive growth fund, then the growth fund may be better for you. If you are seeking growth, and current income is not important, you should have part of your invested dollars in a good growth fund.

GROWTH AND INCOME FUNDS

Growth and income funds seek to combine long-term capital gain and some income by investing in established companies which have a history of steady growth.

You may find in the portfolios of growth and income funds some utility stocks which have both growth and good dividend payments. There also may be convertible corporate bonds. Investing in companies which pay good dividends helps to reduce the volatility of growth and income funds. The dividends will offset some of the occasional downturns. The conservative aspect of the growth and income funds can be observed by comparing the dividend rate with those of growth and aggressive growth funds. In 1989, the average dividend of aggressive growth funds was 1.2 percent; growth funds, 2.9 percent; and growth and income funds, 3.8 percent. If you are not constituted to handle the volatility of aggressive growth or growth funds, then be a little more conservative and think in terms of growth and income.

INCOME FUNDS

The objective of these funds is to primarily make investments which will, within a conservative view, preserve principal at low risk, yet provide steady income and, secondarily, increase capital.

Income funds, also known as equity income funds, invest approximately 50 percent of their assets in income-producing stocks and the other 50 percent usually in convertibles and straight debt instruments.

Comparatively, at the end of 1989, income fund portfolio holdings averaged, including some cash, 62 percent in equities and 38 percent in bonds. Growth and income were 89 percent in equities and 11 percent in bonds, while growth funds were 98 percent in equities, and aggressive growth funds 99 percent in equities.

Income funds are categorized somewhere between growth and income and bond funds. Basically, income funds seek as much income as possible, consistent with reasonable risk and preservation of capital. They are, secondarily, interested in capital growth.

In the category of income funds, there will be convertible securities funds and the newer balanced funds. For the ten-year period 1979 through 1990, income funds were outstanding in their performance, outperforming aggressive growth funds due to strong gains in both stock and bond holdings.

FIXED INCOME FUNDS

Fixed income funds seek to maximize income with the least amount of volatility and risk commensurate with conservation of capital. Because of highly diversified choices, a complete discussion of fixed income funds is covered in Chapter 4.

MONEY MARKET MUTUAL FUNDS

The highest possible current income along with liquidity and capital preservation are the primary objectives of money market mutual funds. In periods of down markets they can be an excellent place to park your money for steady, high return.

Although money market mutual funds have become the most widely held of all mutual funds, they are not insured. However, no one has ever lost a dime investing in money market mutual funds.

These funds provide a constant share price of $1.00 and invest in numerous short-term financial papers, such as repurchase agreements, commercial paper, Eurodollar CDs, U.S. Treasury bills, commercial bank CDs, cash reserves, bankers acceptances, and other treasury securities.

Do not confuse *bank money market funds* with *money market mutual funds*. Although the bank funds are insured, you will receive an average of 1.5 to 2 percent less interest, which is a high price to pay for that insurance considering the outstanding safety record of money market mutual funds. Stringent SEC regulations considerably reduce the risk, if any, of investing in money market mutual funds.

There are different types of money market mutual funds. There are government money funds which invest in treasury bills, in the student loan marketing association (Sallie Mae), in the home loan mortgage corporation, and in repurchase agreements.

Tax-exempt Money Market Mutual Funds

While regular money market funds hold instruments which mature in an average of 44 days, tax-exempt money funds will, generally, hold short-term municipal securities with average maturities of 53 days; government money funds, 49 days.

These tax-exempt money funds are primarily for use by people in high-tax brackets. To compare whether or not you can do better with a taxable money fund as opposed to a tax-free fund, there is a simple formula to determine what the lower tax-free interest rate is worth in taxable dollars. Take the following steps:

Subtract your tax bracket from 100 (*example: 28% from 100 = 72*). Now divide the tax-free interest rate by 72 to determine what taxable rate you need to earn to be equal to the tax-free amount.

Example: Interest on a regular money account is 8.5%. You are considering a tax-free money fund yielding 6%. Assuming a 28% tax bracket, divide 6 (tax-free interest rate) by 72 and you will get .0833% or 8.33% interest on the tax-free money fund. You are better off with the taxable money fund.

Choosing a Money Market Mutual Fund

If you are simply looking for a good money market bank or mutual fund, review each week in your local paper, *Barron's* or the *Wall Street Journal,* the current rates being paid by the 500 or more money market funds available. Bear in mind that the rates quoted are the annual rates which, to achieve, you would have to hold the fund for an entire year. But the same rate all year is highly unlikely. Interest rates fluctuate all during the year.

To select a money market mutual fund, you should choose a money fund, with telephone switch privileges, in the family of mutual funds in which you intend to invest. It is wise to first invest in the money market fund and then, using your telephone switching privileges, transfer your money into the fund or funds of your choice. We will address this in Chapter 9 on strategies.

Most money funds have check writing privileges. However, some have higher minimums than others. Some funds will not honor a check for less than $500. There are others with lower minimums of $250 and even $100. You should determine your check writing needs and select the appropriate money market mutual fund.

In summary, be sure that you request, in your application, telephone switching privileges, wire transfer arrangements for prompt transfer of your funds to your bank account, check writing privileges, and make sure you get prompt responses to your call on the fund company 800 line. Having busy lines when you need prompt attention is not conducive to making switches either to other funds in the family of funds or to money market cash. Also check the prospectus of the money market fund to learn of expenses such as 12b-1 fees, the percentage of management fees, and any other expense ratios. Actually, the larger the fund assets, the lower the percentage of expense, and the fund should pay a higher rate of interest. Table 3-2 provides a checklist for selecting a money market mutual fund including all the things you should consider.

One other thing to watch for: frequently a fund company will waive, for a period of time, its management fee to attract new investors causing its rate of return to be much higher as a result of the waiver. It can be of benefit to you, but keep an eye on the rate of return, as the funds will not likely advise you when they begin to phase in their management fee.

Simulated Money Market Funds

The true no-load money market fund has a constant net asset value of $1.00 per share. There are now global currency funds which act much like a money market fund except the NAV will vary. Because of high interest rates in some foreign countries these funds are a temptation and may show as much as 2 percent more interest than U.S. rates.

These funds should really be considered fixed income or bond funds. The maturity dates of the money instruments in their portfolios may run as long as 365 days as opposed to the much shorter maturities of the no-load money market funds. None of the present international or global income or currency funds are true no-loads.

There is a risk involved in these short-term global income funds which comes about with the fluctuation of the dollar against other currencies. These funds use a complicated hedging technique to protect against the rise of the dollar, which reduces the value of foreign assets for American investors. While the hedging system may work a high percentage of the time, it could backfire due to economic downturns in foreign countries or to political pressures which could force changes in the European monetary system on which hedging techniques are based.

THE NEWER TYPES OF MUTUAL FUNDS

There has been such a proliferation of mutual funds in the last 15 years that some discussion of these other types is necessary. These other types of funds fall into one of the six basic categories listed at the beginning of the chapter. Here is a brief description of funds carrying names other than the six basics.

Asset and Global Asset Allocation Funds

These funds are intended to be conservative, investing in varied types of securities, such as stocks, bonds, precious metals, and some cash. This spreads the risk in a single fund. Some of these funds will start with an even amount in each of the sectors and, recognizing they will not all grow at the same rate, may rebalance the investment in each of the sectors every six or twelve months. These are also known as flexible portfolio funds.

Balanced Funds

Balanced funds will usually invest from 25 percent to 50 percent of their funds in interest-bearing securities

TABLE 3-2: CHOOSING MONEY MARKET MUTUAL FUNDS—A WORKSHEET

Fund Family	Fund Name	(800) Phone	Phone Ex.(Y/N)

Continued

TABLE 3-2: CHOOSING MONEY MARKET MUTUAL FUNDS—A WORKSHEET, Continued

WireTrans. (Y/N)	Other Service(s)	Fee(s)	Exp. Ratio	Investment Min.($) Sub. ($)		Withdraw Min. ($)

—bonds, convertibles, preferred stocks—and the rest in common stocks. These could fall in the categories of income, growth and income, or growth as their objective.

Common Stock Funds

Applies to aggressive growth and growth funds. They invest almost entirely in common stocks.

Index Funds

Some mutual fund companies establish a fund which invests in an index; for example, in the same stocks as the S&P 500 Index. This would be considered an index fund, and it requires no actual management, so expense ratios are very low. Similarly, there are other index funds such as a Pacific index and a European index. In the long-term the market has an up trend and, therefore, an index fund can be a good long-term investment. This is especially true for large institutional buyers, such as pension funds with millions of dollars to invest. Their calculation indicates that the savings on the low management costs are approximately 2 percent over other types of funds and, inasmuch as it is difficult to beat the market by 2 percent, these funds make good sense. There are no-load index funds available for the long-term investor who does not mind the volatility of the market, knowing that the ultimate trend is up.

International and Global Funds

Internationals investing in stock are entirely invested in foreign securities. International bond funds are invested entirely in foreign bonds. Global funds invest in international and U.S. securities. As noted, there are both stock and bond funds among the internationals and the globals.

Multi-Funds

In some instances, a mutual fund family will establish a fund which actually invests in that fund family's other funds. So instead of you investing in, perhaps, five to seven funds in that family, you can invest in one and receive the benefit of five to seven others within the same family of funds. For example, a multi-fund may invest in four common stock funds, two fixed income (bond) funds, and a money market fund. This is well-rounded diversification. It might prove attractive for the young investor just starting out with limited money to invest or for an IRA investment. However, history indicates that multi-funds have not been highly successful, and if you want to start out with one because of limited money, you should switch to something more aggressive as soon as practical.

Regional Funds

Regionals invest 76 percent to 80 percent, possibly more, in stocks within their own region, which can consist of four or five surrounding states or countries.

Sector Funds

There are available low-load and some no-load mutual funds which invest exclusively in one industry sector, such as health care, communications, utilities, and many others. These are aggressive growth funds and are quite volatile.

Social Conscience Funds

These invest in companies which contribute to world peace, to life support products such as medicine, health care, and education, but will avoid investments such as in tobacco, liquor, and gambling stocks. Some will not invest in South Africa.

Value Funds

Fund managers of value funds are constantly looking for companies with low price/earnings ratios and low price/book ratios but with high yielding dividends. Usually the names of these funds will carry the word "value" or "asset." They belong in the growth or growth and income category.

VARIABLE ANNUITIES

Although variable annuities are not a mutual fund, you should be familiar with them because there has been a proliferation of these annuities which allow you to select from several mutual funds in which they invest your premiums. Naturally, the fact that the money you invest is tax deferred seems attractive. However, these are issued by insurance companies, and there is a load in purchasing as well as high management fees. There are several mutual fund companies, and there will be more, now offering a no-load variable annuity with low management costs. The mutual funds developed in each case are "clones" of funds listed on the market, although managed, as a rule, by the same manager of the original fund. Like IRA funds, there is a penalty if you withdraw before age 59-1/2. Unless you can remain in a low cost, no-load variable annuity for at least ten years or more, the tax savings you realize with this type of fund is not worth the cost. You should invest in a good portfolio of mutual funds.

   Although selecting a fund from all the descriptions of no-load mutual funds may seem confusing to you at this point, several selections of portfolios for all age groups in conservative risk, moderate risk, and aggressive risk will be discussed later including descriptions of several investing strategies.

Fixed Income Funds
(Bond Funds)

The objective of fixed income securities is to maximize income with the least amount of volatility and risk commensurate with conservation of capital. Broad examples of fixed income investments are as follows:

Corporate bond funds
Global and International bond funds
GNMA bond funds
Government bond funds
Junk bond funds
Municipal bond funds
Zero-Coupon bond funds

A bond is an engraved certificate indicating that a corporation or a government has borrowed a fixed sum of money and promises to repay it at a future date with a specified rate of interest, usually paid twice per year. Bonds are issued for different time periods: short-term bonds, generally three to seven years; intermediate bonds, seven to ten years; and long-term bonds, over ten years.

In addition, the quality of bonds are rated by different agencies, with Moody's and Standard and Poor's (S&P) the most widely known.

INVESTING IN BOND FUNDS

Conceivably you could, in your lifetime, receive four times as much interest with bond funds as you will spend in interest payments to service a debt. How? With no-load bond funds, you can lend money to banks, governments, and corporations, with maximum returns at reasonable risks.

During periods when inflation begins to ebb, such as 1981 to 1987, bond funds delivered an enviable combination of interest and capital gains, with very low price volatility. The average long-term bond fund grew 17 percent per year for the five-year period 1981 through 1986.

However, for many years bond funds were poor investments due to inflation. Returns fell dramatically, and prices were very volatile. Bond funds grew only 3.3 percent from 1977 to 1981 and, since yields were higher, it means there was loss of principal and purchasing power. Bear in mind that bond funds rise when interest rates drop and lose principal as interest rates rise. If a bond fund yields 10 percent and is selling for $10 per share and it changes one cent in price, that is the equivalent of losing or gaining four days' interest.

Purchasing bond funds is very advantageous over purchasing individual bonds. You will get great diversification and immediate liquidity. No-load bond funds can always be sold at net asset value, with no commission. When an occasional bond defaults it has little effect on a fund, whereas owning an individual bond which defaults can have a more serious effect on your total personal portfolio.

Individual bonds, especially high-grade corporate or government, can always be held until maturity, and you will get your principal back. However, inflation may have eroded the value of that principal over the time you held the bond from the purchase date to maturity. This point will be covered further in Chapter 8.

A bond fund has no specific maturity date, but will hold bonds with similar maturity dates usually stated in the fund's objective. For example, a bond fund whose objective states it will maintain a portfolio of bonds with maturities of between five to seven years makes this an intermediate-term fund. As one of the bonds reaches maturity (for example, a five-year bond), the fund manager will replace it with another five-year bond in order to keep the objective of the fund and have a portfolio with average maturities of five to seven years.

RISKS OF BONDS AND BOND FUNDS

Risk in bonds or bond funds can be controlled by both the quality of the bond as measured by its bond rating and through the maturities you select.

Quality

A bond's quality is measured by its bond rating. Evaluation of the quality or risk is available from Moody's and Standard and Poor's. The lower the rating, the more speculative. The first four ratings are considered investment grade. Below investment grade are the high yield or junk bonds. Ratings are as shown in Table 3-1.

The risk of default is high in *junk bonds* or *junk bond funds*. However, bond mutual funds offer varying degrees of protection from all risks.

Government bonds and government bond funds have no default possibilities but fluctuate in value as interest rates rise and fall.

High-grade corporates are usually *insured bonds* and *insured bond funds* and have no default risk.

TABLE 3-1: BOND RATINGS

	Moody's	*S&P*
Top quality, maximum safety	Aaa	AAA
Very high grade and quality	Aa	AA
High grade, investment quality	A	A
Good grade, medium quality	Baa	BBB
Speculative grade	Ba	BB
Small assurance of continued interest payment	B	B
Default possible	Caa	CCC or CC
Default, partial recovery possible	Ca	C
Default, little recovery possible	C	D

Maturity Risk

The longer the maturity of a bond, the greater the risk. There are two important variables in determining performance: the fund's willingness to protect against price decline by either going to cash equivalents, or by shortening maturities during periods of falling bond prices.

TYPES OF BOND MUTUAL FUNDS

There are eight basic types of no-load bond funds. As with equity and money market mutual funds, each type of bond fund has a different amount of volatility and therefore varied degrees of risk and reward. Following are brief descriptions of each one.

Corporate Bond Funds

Rather than issue more stock, many corporations would rather borrow money by issuing bonds. Such bonds will be given a rating. The rating will be based on the company's history of earning power and stability of operation. If the rating is low, then that corporation is asking you to take a greater degree of risk than a corporation issuing a bond with a higher rating. Under the circumstances, the low-rated bond will pay a higher rate of interest. Corporate bonds may be "called." If the interest rates drop and the corporation can issue bonds at a lower interest rate, they will "call in" the higher yielding bond to save money. Read the prospectus of the bond fund for the callable information to determine the circumstances under which bonds in the portfolio may be called.

Government Bond Funds

There are short-term (0-5 years), intermediate-term (6-15 years), and long-term (15 or more years) government bonds. They are backed by the full faith and credit of the U.S. government. However, they can fluctuate in value according to interest rates. Government bond funds will include government agency securities, treasury bills, treasury notes, and treasury bonds. Check the prospectus of the government bond fund to determine the average maturity. Remember, the longer the maturity, the greater the risk and, usually, the higher the interest.

Table 4-2 will give you an indication of the effect of interest rate movements on government securities.

Zero-Coupon Bond Funds

The most volatile of the bond funds, they are available in both corporate and government. They earn interest but

TABLE 4-2: $10,000 INVESTMENT

*Approximate change in value when interest rates
move up or down 1%*

3 month treasury bill	$25
1-year treasury bill	$100
5-year treasury note	$400
10-year treasury note	$650
30-year treasury note	$1,000
30-year zero-coupon bond	$3,000

do not pay the interest until maturity. Meanwhile, you pay taxes on that earned interest each year. Zero-coupons are sold at a substantial discount, usually to long-term investors with long-term goals, such as a child's college education. There are government target zero-coupon bond funds which have a specific target date of maturity, such as the year 2000, or 2010. These are highly sensitive to interest rates, especially the longer the term and, as with other bonds, may have an erosion of buying power due to inflation when they come due.

Junk Bond Funds

These are low-rated bonds which pay high rates of interest. There have been many defaults during downturns in the economy. They can be very rewarding in bull markets, and if the portfolio is widely diversified, an occasional default will not affect the fund more than 1 or 2 percent. Nevertheless, they carry a high degree of risk.

Global and International Bond Funds

Global funds invest in bonds worldwide, including the U.S. *International bond funds* invest in foreign bonds but not U.S. bonds. Since the investments in these funds are primarily denominated in foreign currencies, exchange rates have a significant impact on total performance. In addition, investments in foreign securities involve special considerations due to more limited information, higher brokerage costs, different accounting standards, thinner trading markets, and the likely impact of foreign taxes on the yield from debt securities.

GNMA Bond Funds

Called "Ginnie Mae," or Government National Mortgage Association, these funds purchase mortgages from banks and savings and loans, pooling them and selling participation certificates to individuals or to mutual funds. The interest and principal are guaranteed by the government GNMA corporation, but when interest rates come down there are usually a large number of individuals who will refinance their mortgages, and the high yields do a vanishing act. If interest rates go up, individuals do not refinance, but the principal of your GNMA fund will decrease in value just as it does in other bond funds.

Municipal Bond Funds

These funds, as a rule, yield lower interest rates because they are exempt from the federal income tax. These bonds are issued by states, cities, and municipalities for road and highway improvement, building schools and hospitals. There are rare occasions when a default will occur. There are also long-term municipals, and they will fluctuate in price with interest rate swings. If you own a state municipal bond fund in the state in which you live, it will also probably be exempt from your state income taxes.

Bonds and bond funds are not for buying and holding indefinitely. If you feel that you can detect when interest rates have reached a peak, that might be a good time to invest in bonds which will then increase in value as interest rates decline. However, stock funds will do better than bonds when interest rates are declining. The advantages of no-load bond funds are the same as all other no-load funds: wide diversification, professional management, and liquidity. Since bonds are interest-rate sensitive, you can lose a lot of money when interest rates are rising.

Getting Started with Fund Investing

As stated in Chapter 1, there is some homework involved in beginning your mutual fund investments, so use your self-discipline to set aside regular time to do a bit of research. Once you understand the fundamentals, as outlined in this book, you will find that making a selection is not as complicated as it seems at first.

After making your selection, it becomes a simple matter to ascertain your fund's progress on a weekly basis by checking the financial pages of any large metropolitan newspaper or, perhaps, you may wish to subscribe to the weekly, *Barron's*. In addition to weekly coverage, *Barron's* also publishes, once each quarter, a full report, including five- and ten-year performances of all mutual funds. The report is compiled by Lipper Analytical Services, Inc., which tracks all mutual funds.

GETTING STARTED

To get started, you need to make two important decisions:

1. You must decide on your *objective*—a new car, a new home, a child's education, and/or retirement.

2. You need to decide if you have a high or low tolerance for *risk*. The younger you are, the more risk you can afford to take to achieve your goals. Table 5-1 provides a general guide for different risk levels depending on career status.

TABLE 5-1: RISK LEVELS

Career Stage	*Risk Tolerance*
Early	High
Mid	High
Late	Moderate
Retirement	Low

What type of funds should you start with? Let us say that young people with moderate income, investing for the long term, should be aggressive. You do not need income from your investment, you do not need liquidity, but you will have liquidity with no-load mutual funds in the event you need it. Therefore, you should be thinking in terms of aggressive growth funds and growth funds, including international stock funds. As you get older, your selection of funds will become gradually more moderate. Illustrations of a number of portfolio choices for all ages, including aggressive, moderate and conservative, are covered in Chapter 8.

In making your first fund selections, however, you may wish to start out with a more conservative approach and select a fund or funds whose stated objectives meet your own risk tolerance.

Next, call or write the fund companies having funds which interest you, and ask for a prospectus on each fund that meets your objective. In Chapter 6 you'll learn how

TABLE 5-2: WHAT $1,000 DEPOSITED ANNUALLY WILL GROW TO IN A GIVEN NUMBER OF YEARS

% increase compounded annually

Year	5%	6%	7%	8%	9%	10%	11%	12%	13%	14%	15%	16%	17%	18%	19%	20%
1	1,050	1,060	1,070	1,080	1,090	1,100	1,110	1,120	1,130	1,140	1,150	1,160	1,170	1,180	1,190	1,200
2	2,153	2,184	2,215	2,246	2,278	2,310	2,342	2,374	2,407	2,440	2,473	2,506	2,539	2,572	2,606	2,640
3	3,310	3,375	3,440	3,506	3,573	3,641	3,710	3,779	3,850	3,921	3,993	4,066	4,141	4,215	4,291	4,368
4	4,526	4,637	4,751	4,867	4,985	5,105	5,228	5,353	5,480	5,610	5,742	5,877	6,014	6,154	6,297	6,442
5	5,802	5,975	6,153	6,336	6,523	6,716	6,913	7,115	7,323	7,536	7,754	7,977	8,207	8,442	8,683	8,930
6	7,142	7,394	7,654	7,923	8,200	8,487	8,783	9,089	9,405	9,730	10,067	10,414	10,772	11,142	11,523	11,916
7	8,549	8,897	9,260	9,637	10,028	10,436	10,859	11,300	11,757	12,233	12,727	13,240	13,773	14,327	14,902	15,499
8	10,027	10,491	10,978	11,488	12,021	12,579	13,164	13,776	14,416	15,085	15,786	16,519	17,285	18,086	18,923	19,799
9	11,578	12,181	12,816	13,487	14,193	14,937	15,722	16,549	17,420	18,337	19,304	20,321	21,393	22,521	23,709	24,959
10	13,207	13,972	14,784	15,645	16,560	17,531	18,561	19,655	20,814	22,045	23,349	24,733	26,200	27,755	29,404	31,150
11	14,917	15,870	16,888	17,977	19,141	20,384	21,713	23,133	24,650	26,271	28,002	29,850	31,824	33,931	36,180	38,581
12	16,713	17,882	19,141	20,495	21,953	23,523	25,212	27,029	28,985	31,089	33,352	35,786	38,404	41,219	44,244	47,497
13	18,599	20,015	21,550	23,215	25,019	26,975	29,095	31,393	33,883	36,581	39,505	42,672	46,103	49,818	53,841	58,196
14	20,579	22,276	24,129	26,152	28,361	30,772	33,405	36,280	39,417	42,842	46,580	50,660	55,110	59,965	65,261	71,035
15	22,657	24,673	26,888	29,324	32,003	34,950	38,190	41,753	45,672	49,980	54,717	59,925	65,649	71,939	78,850	86,442
16	24,840	27,213	29,840	32,750	35,974	39,545	43,501	47,884	52,739	58,118	64,075	70,673	77,979	86,068	95,022	104,931
17	27,132	29,906	32,999	36,450	40,301	44,599	49,396	54,750	60,725	67,394	74,836	83,141	92,406	102,740	114,266	127,117
18	29,539	32,760	36,379	40,446	45,018	50,159	55,939	62,440	69,749	77,969	87,212	97,603	109,285	122,414	137,166	153,740
19	32,066	35,786	39,995	44,762	50,160	56,275	63,203	71,052	79,947	90,025	101,444	114,380	129,033	145,628	164,418	185,688
20	34,719	38,993	43,865	49,423	55,765	63,002	71,265	80,699	91,470	103,768	117,810	133,841	152,139	173,021	196,847	224,026
21	37,505	42,392	48,006	54,457	61,873	70,403	80,214	91,503	104,491	119,436	136,632	156,415	179,172	205,345	235,438	270,031
22	40,430	45,996	52,436	59,893	68,532	78,543	90,148	103,603	119,205	137,297	158,276	182,601	210,801	243,487	281,362	325,237
23	43,502	49,816	57,177	65,765	75,790	87,497	101,174	117,155	135,831	157,659	183,168	212,978	247,808	288,494	336,010	391,484
24	46,727	53,865	62,249	72,106	83,701	97,347	113,413	132,334	154,620	180,871	211,793	248,214	291,105	341,603	401,042	470,981
25	50,113	58,156	67,676	78,954	92,324	108,182	126,999	149,334	175,850	207,333	244,712	289,088	341,763	404,272	478,431	566,377

Source: Handbook for No-load Fund Investors

money will compound to $108,182 in 25 years. If you invest $2,000 per year in an IRA account with a growth mutual fund, it would be worth $216,364 and would have been tax-deferred all during that 25-year period.

Table 5-3 will show you how a *single* lump sum investment of $10,000 will grow at various rates of return over a given number of years.

I bring these Tables to your attention to illustrate how the power of compounding money will provide you with a potentially large retirement fund. However, now look at Table 5-4 on page 56. This Table points out the one form of resistance in developing your portfolio: *inflation.* What you require to live on today will be affected by inflation over the years until retirement, or any other objective, such as saving for a home, for a child's education, or any other major expenditure.

To calculate how much money you will need at retirement, first determine how much you spend now. Multiply that figure by the adjustment factor in the chart on page 54. Find the correct adjustment factor by first going down the left column until you come to the number of years until you will retire; then move across the columns until you are in the column with the inflation rate you feel is safe to assume. For example, if you need $2,000 per month today and will retire in 20 years, and expect 5 percent yearly inflation rate, you will need $5,300 per month ($2,000 x 2.65) at retirement to maintain your current standard of living.

Investing steadily over the long term is certainly the right way to achieve your goals, and one way to do that is known as dollar cost averaging, which reduces volatility during the long-term period of your investments. We will discuss dollar cost averaging and other investment strategies in a later chapter.

TABLE 5-3: WHAT $10,000 WILL BE WORTH IN A GIVEN NUMBER OF YEARS

% increase compounded annually

Year	5%	6%	7%	8%	9%	10%	11%	12%	13%	14%	15%	16%	17%	18%	19%	20%
1	10,500	10,600	10,700	10,800	10,900	11,000	11,100	11,200	11,300	11,400	11,500	11,600	11,700	11,800	11,900	12,000
2	11,025	11,236	11,449	11,664	11,881	12,100	12,321	12,544	12,769	12,996	13,225	13,456	13,689	13,924	14,161	14,400
3	11,576	11,910	12,250	12,597	12,950	13,310	13,676	14,049	14,429	14,815	15,209	15,609	16,016	16,430	16,852	17,280
4	12,155	12,625	13,108	13,605	14,116	14,641	15,181	15,735	16,305	16,890	17,490	18,106	18,739	19,388	20,053	20,736
5	12,763	13,382	14,026	14,693	15,386	16,105	16,851	17,623	18,424	19,254	20,114	21,003	21,924	22,878	23,864	24,883
6	13,401	14,185	15,007	15,869	16,771	17,716	18,704	19,738	20,820	21,950	23,131	24,364	25,652	26,996	28,398	29,860
7	14,071	15,036	16,058	17,138	18,280	19,487	20,762	22,107	23,526	25,023	26,600	28,262	30,012	31,855	33,793	35,832
8	14,775	15,938	17,182	18,509	19,926	21,436	23,045	24,760	26,584	28,526	30,590	32,784	35,115	37,589	40,214	42,998
9	15,513	16,895	18,385	19,990	21,719	23,579	25,580	27,731	30,040	32,519	35,179	38,030	41,084	44,355	47,854	51,598
10	16,289	17,908	19,672	21,589	23,674	25,937	28,394	31,058	33,946	37,072	40,456	44,114	48,068	52,338	56,947	61,917
11	17,103	18,983	21,049	23,316	25,804	28,531	31,518	34,785	38,359	42,262	46,524	51,173	56,240	61,759	67,767	74,301
12	17,959	20,122	22,522	25,182	28,127	31,384	34,985	38,960	43,345	48,179	53,503	59,360	65,801	72,876	80,642	89,161
13	18,856	21,329	24,098	27,196	30,658	34,523	38,833	43,635	48,980	54,924	61,528	68,858	76,987	85,994	95,964	106,993
14	19,799	22,609	25,785	29,372	33,417	37,975	43,104	48,871	55,348	62,613	70,757	79,875	90,075	101,472	114,198	128,392
15	20,789	23,966	27,590	31,722	36,425	41,772	47,846	54,736	62,543	71,379	81,371	92,655	105,387	119,737	135,895	154,070
16	21,829	25,404	29,522	34,259	39,703	45,950	53,109	61,304	70,673	81,372	93,576	107,480	123,303	141,290	161,715	184,884
17	22,920	26,928	31,588	37,000	43,276	50,545	58,951	68,660	79,861	92,765	107,613	124,677	144,265	166,722	192,441	221,861
18	24,066	28,543	33,799	39,960	47,171	55,599	65,436	76,900	90,243	105,752	123,755	144,625	168,790	196,733	229,005	266,233
19	25,270	30,256	36,165	43,157	51,417	61,159	72,633	86,128	101,974	120,557	142,318	167,765	197,484	232,144	272,516	319,480
20	26,533	32,071	38,697	46,610	56,044	67,275	80,623	96,463	115,231	137,435	163,665	194,608	231,056	273,930	324,294	383,376
21	27,860	33,996	41,406	50,338	61,088	74,002	89,492	108,038	130,211	156,676	188,215	225,745	270,336	323,238	385,910	460,051
22	29,253	36,035	44,304	54,365	66,586	81,403	99,336	121,003	147,138	178,610	216,447	261,864	316,293	381,421	459,233	552,061
23	30,715	38,197	47,405	58,715	72,579	89,543	110,263	135,523	166,266	203,616	248,915	303,762	370,062	450,076	546,487	662,474
24	32,251	40,489	50,724	63,412	79,111	98,497	122,392	151,786	187,881	232,122	286,252	352,364	432,973	531,090	650,320	794,968
25	33,864	42,919	54,274	68,485	86,231	108,347	135,855	170,001	212,305	264,619	329,190	408,742	506,578	626,686	773,881	953,962

Source: Handbook for No-load Fund Investors

TABLE 5-4: HOW MUCH MONEY WILL YOU NEED?

	Inflation Rates				
	5%	8%	10%	12%	15%
Years To Retirement	*Adjustment Rates*				
10	1.63	2.16	2.59	3.11	4.05
11	1.71	2.33	2.85	3.48	4.65
12	1.80	2.52	3.14	3.90	5.34
13	1.89	2.72	3.45	4.36	6.15
14	1.98	2.94	3.80	4.89	7.08
15	2.08	3.17	4.18	5.47	8.14
16	2.18	3.43	4.60	6.13	9.36
17	2.29	3.70	5.05	6.87	10.77
18	2.41	4.00	5.58	7.69	12.38
19	2.53	4.32	6.12	8.61	14.23
20	2.65	4.66	6.73	9.65	16.37
21	2.79	5.03	7.40	10.80	18.82
22	2.93	5.44	8.14	12.10	21.64
23	3.07	5.87	8.95	13.55	24.89
24	3.23	6.34	9.85	15.18	28.63
25	3.39	6.85	10.83	17.00	32.92
26	3.56	7.40	11.92	19.04	37.86
27	3.73	7.99	13.11	21.32	43.54
28	3.92	8.63	14.42	23.88	50.07
29	4.12	9.32	15.86	26.75	57.58
30	4.32	10.06	17.45	29.96	66.22
31	4.54	10.87	19.19	33.56	76.14
32	4.76	11.74	21.22	37.58	87.57
33	5.00	12.68	23.23	42.09	100.70
34	5.25	13.69	25.55	47.14	115.80
35	5.52	14.79	28.10	52.80	113.18

Understanding the Prospectus

There was a time when a mutual fund prospectus contained so much technical detail, as required by the Securities and Exchange Commission (SEC), that it took a highly skilled lawyer to figure it out. It just was not for the average investor.

All that has been changed, and the prospectus is now much simpler and is a definite *must* for you to read. *Investigate before investing.*

The SEC requires that the prospectus provide you with "full and fair disclosure" of all information relevant to your potential investment. It includes information on whether or not the fund has any lawsuits against it, the experience and length of service of its managers, management fees, a complete description of the fund's objectives in clear detail, types of services, minimum and subsequent investment amounts, etc.

The SEC has recommended that the prospectus follow a basic form which most funds comply with, but with occasional variations. Following are the major sections and a brief summary of their contents.

SECTIONS OF THE PROSPECTUS

The Cover Page

This includes the fund name, objective, and date of prospectus. (Be sure to obtain the most recent, preferably less than one year old.) This cover page may also contain the fund's address, phone number, minimum initial investment, and whether it is a load or no-load fund.

There may be warnings, such as unusually high expenses or special risk factors described in detail inside the prospectus. The SEC further protects you by not allowing the fund to use a deceptive name. In other words, the fund name must be somewhat descriptive of its objective.

Synopsis or Highlights

This gives a short summary of the prospectus but possibly may be omitted if the prospectus is short. If included, it highlights the significant features of the offering: the objectives, policies, special considerations, and risk factors. This information should be read carefully. Most of the funds will give you page references to where the complete description of the various features can be found.

Fee Schedule

The fee schedule explains all the costs in connection with purchase and ownership of a mutual fund. The fee schedule found in the prospectus is usually an abbreviation of one found in the "Statement of Additional Information" discussed later in this chapter.

The true no-load fund shows shareholder transactions costs as follows:

Sales load to purchaser	None
Sales load on reinvested dividends	None
Deferred sales charge	None
Exchange fees	None

Restated annual fund operating expenses
net of expense reimbursement

Management fee	0.68%
12b-1 fee	None
Other expenses	0.29%
Total operating expense after expense reimbursement	0.97%

Note that this true, no-load does not have any load fees, deferred or exchange fees, or 12b-1 fees. Management fees and expenses usually run about 1 percent in well-managed equity funds, less in fixed income funds. You should select funds with no more than 1 percent in total management and expense fees.

When comparing the above with no-load funds having 12b-1 and/or redemption fees or with load funds having a front-end commission along with a 12b-1 fee, you will find considerable difference in the cost of operating these funds, reducing the return on your planned investment.

Condensed Financial Information

The per-share income and capital changes are required by the SEC to be shown for the latest ten years or the life of the fund. In Table 6-1 you will see one fund's historical results using per share amounts, which gives you the most revealing perspective on the fund's investment results. The chart is from the audited prospectus of a well-known fund.

TABLE 6-1: CONDENSED FINANCIAL INFORMATION

The following information has been audited by independent accountants, whose report appears in the Statement of Additional Information. This information should be read in conjunction with the audited financial statements appearing in the Fund's 1990 Annual Report to Shareholders and in the Statement of Additional Information.

	Year Ended June 30									
	1990	1989	1988	1987	1986	1985	1984	1983	1982	1981
PER SHARE DATA										
Net Asset Value –										
Beginning of Year	$8.880	$7.978	$8.854	$9.103	$8.421	$7.297	$8.968	$6.576	$7.053	$7.911
OPERATIONS										
Investment Income	0.450	0.485	0.414	0.403	0.512	0.516	0.583	0.486	0.649	0.648
Expenses	0.069	0.065	0.064	0.063	0.066	0.055	0.057	0.050	0.044	0.055
Net Investment Income	0.381	0.420	0.350	0.340	0.446	0.461	0.526	0.436	0.605	0.593
Net Realized and Unrealized										
Gain (Loss) on Investments	1.429	1.014	(0.513)	0.828	2.610	1.805	(0.694)	2.993	(0.502)	0.037
Total from Operations	1.810	1.434	(0.163)	1.168	3.056	2.266	(0.168)	3.429	0.103	0.630
DISTRIBUTIONS										
Net Investment Income	(0.400)	(0.390)	(0.360)	(0.360)	(0.480)	(0.480)	(0.540)	(0.480)	(0.580)	(0.560)
Net Realized Gain	(0.897)	(0.142)	(0.353)	(1.057)	(1.894)	(0.662)	(0.963)	(0.557)	0.000	(0.928)
Total Distributions	(1.297)	(0.532)	(0.713)	(1.417)	(2.374)	(1.142)	(1.503)	(1.037)	(0.580)	(1.488)
Net Change in Net Asset Value ...	0.513	0.902	(0.876)	(0.249)	0.682	1.124	(1.671)	2.392	(0.477)	(0.858)
Net Asset Value –										
End of Year	$9.393	$8.880	$7.978	$8.854	$9.103	$8.421	$7.297	$8.968	$6.576	$7.053
RATIOS										
Ratio of Expenses to										
Average Net Assets	0.76%	0.78%	0.78%	0.74%	0.71%	0.68%	0.64%	0.63%	0.65%	0.66%
Ratio of Net Investment Income										
to Average Net Assets	4.14%	5.08%	4.29%	3.96%	4.85%	5.72%	5.92%	5.48%	8.81%	7.09%
Portfolio Turnover Rate*	132%	124%	148%	195%	160%	54%	54%	57%	72%	110%
Shares Outstanding at End of Year										
(000 Omitted)	60,938	44,996	47,753	50,974	37,552	29,609	25,026	24,824	22,555	23,344

*For years ended prior to 1985, long-term U.S. Government Securities were excluded when computing the portfolio turnover rate.

General Description of the Fund

This section will give you a detailed overview of the fund's types of investments, policies, and objectives. You should read this information over very carefully because it has great value to you in determining if the fund's objectives coincide with your own. The fund's objectives will be such things as *growth, preservation of capital, and income.* The policy statement differs from the objective because it will state how the fund expects to meet the objective. For example, the fund may purchase only stocks which have paid dividends for a given period of time, or buy a mixture of stocks and bonds with good income returns. The general description also tells what the fund is permitted to do and what it is not permitted to do, such as *selling short or borrowing money, or writing put and call options.*

The example of an objective shown as Figure 6-1 states that the fund will primarily provide long-term capital growth (the what) and income will be secondary. The policy example tells you "the how"—at least 80% of the assets will be in equity securities of related industries.

FIGURE 6-1: SAMPLE ABSTRACTS OF FUND OBJECTIVES AND POLICIES

INVESTMENT OBJECTIVE:

The fund seeks to provide long-term capital growth

(The "Fund") is a no-load, open-end diversified investment company with five Portfolios: Energy, Gold and Precious Metals, Health Care, Service Economy and Technology. The objective of the Fund is to provide long-term capital growth. Although a Portfolio may provide dividend income to a limited extent, current income will be secondary to the Fund's primary objective of achieving capital appreciation. There is no assurance that the Fund will achieve its stated objective. The investment objective of the Fund is fundamental and so cannot be changed without the approval of a majority of the Fund's shareholders.

INVESTMENT POLICIES:

Each Portfolio invests in industry-specific common stocks

Under normal circumstances, at least 80% of a Portfolio's assets will be invested in the equity securities (common stocks and securities convertible into common stocks) of companies in a particular industry or group of related industries and, in the case of the Gold and Precious Metals Portfolio, in gold or other precious metal bullion and coins. A common stock or other equity security will generally be considered appropriate for a given Portfolio if, as determined by the investment adviser, at least 50% of the company's assets, revenues or net income are related to or derived from the industry or industries designated for a Portfolio.

Occasionally you will receive a prospectus in which several funds are described. In these cases, the several funds may have the same objective or perhaps just the same manager. When several funds are included in one prospectus there are savings in such things as printing costs and SEC filing fees. This is good because these savings are passed along to the shareholder through lower cost of operations.

Fund Management

Unlike most corporate management, mutual funds, even though owned by their shareholders, are not generally run by their officers but by an outside company known as the investment adviser. The prospectus will give you all the details regarding the adviser, including name, address, experience, and it will give you the name of the transfer and dividend paying agent. Advisory fees are indicated, as well as commissions paid for purchase and sale of securities.

Capital Stock and Other Securities

This section informs you of your voting rights, redemption of shares, restrictions, if any, on selling your shares, dividends, distributions, and tax consequences.

How to Purchase Shares

The procedures for purchasing shares are discussed here. It will tell you about telephone switch privileges, any sales charges, distribution fees, and the minimum and subsequent investment amounts. There will be an application with the prospectus. It is not complicated to complete.

Pending Legal Proceedings

If there are any such proceedings, this information must be disclosed here. Such proceedings will not usually affect your investment.

STATEMENT OF ADDITIONAL INFORMATION

There is another document called the "Statement of Additional Information." This will provide less important, though more detailed, information and, if you are a potential investor, the fund will send you this information *only if you ask for it*. Some of the sections covered in the prospectus will probably be duplicated here. A complete description of the advisor, management fees, and unaudited per share data and ratios are spelled out in this statement.

Should you have a problem understanding anything in the prospectus or the statement of additional information, call the fund's 800-number and discuss the item with a customer service person. If you do not find that person able to explain the subject to your satisfaction, ask for a supervisor or even the fund manager. Remember: the only dumb question is the one you do not ask.

Making the Right No-Load
Fund Selection

As I mentioned earlier, there are individual no-load funds, and there are "families" of funds. Most fund families offer a wide and diversified selection of funds which is, ultimately, important to your investment program. Investing in one family of funds gives you the opportunity to select from the wide variety of fund types—stocks, bonds, international funds, precious metals, sector funds, money market funds, and possibly others—plus it gives you the added advantage of switching from one fund to another within the family with just a phone call. Most no-load funds do not charge for telephone switching. Some fund families, however, do have some limitations such as the number of times per year you can switch. Again, check the prospectus.

When looking into families of funds, compare their management fees. Remember to avoid those extra fees so that you invest only in the "true" no-load fund where your only cost is the management fee and miscellaneous operating expenses.

Once you have decided on a fund family, compare the funds you are interested in by calling the fund company and obtaining information from the customer service representative and, of course, asking for a prospectus. Find out how long the manager has been running the fund. Although experience does count for something, remember that past performance is no guarantee of future success.

The greatest variation in performance will be in equity funds (those investing in stocks). Check the histories of the stock funds in each family you consider to see if performance has been consistent over time. Give preference to funds which have the best records in bear markets. This is an indication of good, steady, performance and is certainly the goal of the long-term investor. A more detailed discussion on what to look for in a fund family follows.

CRITERIA FOR SELECTING A FUND FAMILY

By now you're asking yourself, "which family of funds do I choose?" Believe it or not, this is more important than asking "which fund do I choose?" There has been such a proliferation of mutual funds, with fund families having such varying strengths and diversity of funds, that you should examine the funds within fund families in sequence. First examining equity funds and then the bond funds.

First look at aggressive growth funds. Only a small number of fund families have outstanding performers in this category. Make a list of these funds and their performance over time. Next look at growth and growth and income funds. Most fund families have shown reasonably good results with these types of funds.

Now, compare the bond funds in the fund families. While looking at bond funds, you want to evaluate your own position by answering two questions.

1. What tax bracket are you in? If you're in a high tax bracket, you might want to look at tax-free bond funds. I'll explain why later in Chapter 8.

2. Are you leaning toward taxable or tax-free bond funds? *(Again, bond funds for younger individuals and for those not yet approaching retirement years are usually not appropriate.)* Most families of funds will have long-term bond funds, but not too many have short-term tax-free or taxable funds to which you might wish to switch during adverse market conditions.

Next in your search for a fund family, look into money market funds. There are three types: general money market funds, government money market funds, and tax-free money market funds. If you find a fund family with all three, it's a big advantage.

Also look for both stock and bond international funds within a fund family. We are going more and more to an international economy, and you want to be well-positioned in the fund family you choose.

If you find specialty or sector funds in the family, this can be a plus. However, these funds can be volatile and high risk.

Finally, remember to look for no-load funds in the family. Some load or low-load, in fact, loads of any kind among no-loads, can be an inhibiting factor. You also want to make sure the fund family has telephone switch privileges. This is important to help you to diversify, reduce volatility in adverse markets, and move to more aggressive funds in bull markets. We will be discussing these strategies and others in Chapter 9.

CRITERIA FOR SELECTING AGGRESSIVE GROWTH FUNDS

In Chapter 3 we described the six basic types of funds, beginning with aggressive growth funds. If you have decided to purchase shares of aggressive growth funds, you should consider the following:

- *Past history of performance.* Look at five-year to ten-year studies of the average total return per year. This includes growth combined with reinvested dividends. There are new funds arriving on the scene every year and some with potentially good prospects, but as a beginner stay with the older, more established funds.

- *Fund management.* Look for excellent *intermediate* as well as *short-term* performance. Find out how long the manager has been running the fund and, if available, determine how he or she managed during both bull and bear markets.

- *Fund size.* Compare fund sizes. That is, look at total assets under management. Some funds, through efficient management, grow to be quite large and at a certain point will close to new investors. In the opinion of management, these funds have become unwieldy and because of their policy statement, may hold large amounts of stock in a few major corporations. Any substantial sales they make could reduce the price of the fund. In many cases, when a fund grows too large, management will start a new fund with the same objective; cloning the original fund. Smaller funds, with greater maneuverability are apt to gain more than the larger funds. As an example, my notes from a 1990 seminar indicate that during 1989 the top performing 25 funds in both load and no-load consisted of 16 funds with assets under $50 million, six funds between $50 million and $300 million, and three funds over $300 million. The next 25 funds with assets of $700 million or more performed less well than the first group of 25 funds.

Of course, the smaller funds may not always perform well if management is inferior. By the same token, there have been outstanding managers who can continue to develop good performance with the larger funds in spite of the unwieldy size.

- *Cash position.* All funds need to have some cash position in order to make redemptions. However, aggressive growth funds should be fully invested during bull markets but should keep more cash instruments in the portfolio during bear markets.

- *Positive cash flow versus negative cash flow.* A fund with greater positive cash flow is more likely to have better performance; more money is coming in than going out for redemptions. This gives the manager more latitude to add to good performing holdings or take advantage of inviting new issues instead of having to decide to sell some holdings to purchase others.

All of these factors are important to the successful performance of an aggressive growth fund, notwithstanding unanticipated changes in world events and severe economic problems.

CRITERIA FOR SELECTING LESS VOLATILE, MORE CONSERVATIVE FUNDS

Unlike aggressive growth funds, there is a different criterion for selecting growth, growth income, income, and balanced funds. These are the funds for long-term investing, and while we have been concerned with the size and cash inflow of aggressive funds we want to look more into long-term performance of these more conservative types of funds. It is important to look at the results in both bull and bear markets if the fund you are considering is old enough to have experienced both. Look up the fund record during the last year of a bear market and the most recent bull market; then compare that with similar funds to determine which performed better under both conditions.

The ideal growth fund will not pay dividends and will grow steadily, eliminating taxes until you sell some shares. Many individuals shop for yields especially when interest rates go down. This is okay when comparing certificates of deposits but not when selecting funds. You should look for total return instead: the sum of growth and reinvested dividends (yields). The best returns, then, will usually be found in growth and income or balanced funds which invest partly in stocks paying good dividends and bonds with good interest rates.

Be sure to check the beta, which is the indication of volatility (risk) compared with the S&P 500. These types of funds, should have betas of less than one; less volatile than the S&P 500. The average growth fund has a beta of .88; the average growth income fund has a beta of .76; the average income fund has a beta of .54 and the average balanced fund has a beta of .55. When you are comparing two like funds which have a close similarity in track record, choose the one with the lower beta for less volatility.

Again, check the expense ratios and management fees in the prospectus. Once more, remember that, in the long run, 12b-1 fees, loads, low-loads, and redemption fees become a real "drag" on the growth of your no-load investment. For example, an index fund which buys the same stocks as those in the S&P 500, has a low management fee, and a low expense ratio of only .25 percent, a great deal less, about 75 percent less, than the average equity fund. However, instead of this fund being equal to the results of the S&P 500, it grew 5 percent less in five years than the S&P 500. It becomes obvious that if a low .25 percent fee has that much effect on total performance of this index fund, then a fund with additional charges plus higher management fees will have a much more negative effect on that fund. Usually expense ratios are found in the prospectus headed "per share income and capital change."

In summary, if the fund has an outstanding growth record and the same manager over a period of time, then the chances are better for continuation of that record than with a fund whose history is not as good. Bear in mind that no one has a "crystal ball" that can predict which fund or funds will be the next ten-year winners. Instead, select a fund family and no-load funds most suitable to your own objectives and which are not over-priced in fees and expenses.

FUND FAMILIES AND YOUR TAX-SHELTERED INVESTMENTS

A good family of funds is, without doubt, the best possible way to invest your tax-deferred plan. The family of funds you select should offer considerable diversity and telephone switch privileges to make it easy to manage your retirement program. As you approach the retirement years, you will want to switch from the more aggressive funds in your portfolio to more conservative funds. A simple telephone call will do the trick.

One word of caution. Avoid trying to "second guess" the market by switching your money in and out of different funds. It is a temptation to want to switch to a fund which has been especially "hot" during the past 12 months, but remember the old story of the tortoise and the hare. We will discuss market timing in Chapter 9.

In the final analysis, it pays to analyze and select a widely diversified family of no-load funds in the beginning, with telephone switch privileges and to stick with that family for your tax-sheltered investing. Do not, however, invest your IRA or Keogh in tax-free bond funds. You are already tax sheltered, and such an investment would lead to paying taxes on your tax-free dividends when you draw them out.

In recommending that you remain with one family of funds for your tax-sheltered investments, this does not necessarily imply that you remain with the same family for your other mutual fund investments.

While it is easier to remain with one family of funds to get the advantage of continuous paperwork recording the entire history of your investments, this does not preclude switching to a fund or funds in another family. When making such a switch, with your IRA or Keogh, contact the fund family you wish to switch to and ask for 1) the prospectus of the fund in which you wish to invest, 2) an application, and 3) a transfer form. Then let that fund company make the switch for you.

By doing the switching in this manner, you can, legally, make as many switches per year as you wish. If you decide to have the funds sent to you by the company in which you are invested, you *must* reinvest within 60 days, and then you can make no additional switches for 12 months. If you do not reinvest within the 60-day period, you will pay taxes on the full amount of the withdrawal, and if you are under 59-1/2 years of age, you will pay a 10 percent penalty.

Mary, Mary, Quite Contrary, How Does My Money Grow?

Tax-sheltered money has a tremendous advantage over the investments on which you pay income taxes. Compounding the growth is much faster and greater, but what is your risk tolerance? Are you a conservative investor? A moderate investor or an aggressive investor? Let me help you with this decision? Take a look at these figures for tax sheltered income:

- $2,000 per year invested in your IRA at 5 percent per year for 40 years will equal $242,000.

- $2,000 per year invested in your IRA at 10 percent per year for 40 years will equal $885,000.

- $2,000 per year invested in your IRA at 15 percent per year for 40 years will equal $3,558,000.

Before you decide your risk tolerance, take a look at some additional figures:

COMPOUND ANNUAL RETURN FOR 64 YEARS WITH INCOME REINVESTED

Common stocks from the S&P 500	10.3%
Corporate bonds	5.2%
Government long term bonds	4.6%
Treasury bills	3.6%
Inflation (*Consumer Price Index*)	3.1%

This covers the period January 1, 1926 through December 31, 1989. Subtracting the annual average rate of inflation from the average rate of returns on the various investments leaves you a return of 7.2 percent on stock, 2.1 percent on corporate bonds, 1.5 percent on government long term bonds and only .5 percent ahead of inflation with Treasury bills. You can now review Table 5-4 on inflation at the end of Chapter 5. Now review Table 5-3, "What $1,000 deposited annually will grow to in a given number of year." If you can deposit $2,000 in your IRA, just double the figures on the chart.

To help you determine your risk tolerance and how you should invest your tax-sheltered money, I will illustrate several varied portfolios for different age groups in Chapter 8. They may be of help in determining how to allocate your funds at different stages of your life.

The earlier you start your tax-sheltered investing, the more you will have in retirement. It is never too early to start an IRA. Those who start young and are consistent in making their annual contribution until age 65 will have a sizeable amount of money at retirement. Additionally, make your IRA or Keogh contribution as early in the year as possible so as to tax shelter the income for the greatest part of the year.

SUMMARY

Following, in summary, are rules for weathering the storm of market investments.

- Have confidence in the long-term quality mutual fund investment. If you have made a sensible investment, have patience. It will work.

- The long-term, steady investor, will be successful and will also sleep well at night.

- Remember, unexpected events can occur any time, which can have a temporary adverse effect.

- Keep your moods and emotions in check when investing. Do not let them go to extremes.

- Any severe problem in an industry can result in a drop in price of a strong company as well as a weak one.

- There are challenges to the modern investor which our fathers never faced. For example, our current technology, instant communication, program trading, all tend to make many investors want to jump from one fund to another just because a fund is "hot" at the moment. This can work against you and your best interests. A good balanced portfolio, with steady additional investment over the long term, is still best for most investors.

- There are times, of course, when a mutual fund should be sold or exchanged. If you have compared other funds with the same objectives as the one you chose, then continue to make the same comparison from time to time. If your fund drops into the bottom half of all those you compare it with, sell it.

- Mutual funds should never be sold on the same basis as individual stocks or bonds. A stock or bond may have doubled or tripled in price over a period of time, and you will sell it to protect your gain. Mutual fund managers are already doing this for you in their portfolios: buying new stocks and selling others, reinvesting the profits for greater long-term results.

- Do not gamble with things like options and futures. These are high risk gambles. Avoid loads and other charges and, last but not least, do not invest in anything you do not understand. Investigate before investing—read the prospectus.

- Being a member of the NASD board of arbitrators, I am quite often amazed at how naive an investor can be about risk and how little a broker emphasizes risk, but prefers to hand the client a prospectus, which the client fails to read. Then, if the investment goes bad, the client brings the broker before an arbitration panel claiming the broker caused the loss. *Let the buyer beware. . . read the prospectus. Never invest in anything you do not understand.*

Retirement Portfolio Programs

You have just completed Chapter 7 which has given you something to think about when selecting a fund family and fund type in relation to being an aggressive investor, a moderate investor, or a conservative investor. The type of fund you select, of course, depends on your age, family status, total objective in planning your retirement program, or if you are already in retirement.

In this chapter we will illustrate a choice of portfolios of no-load mutual funds for four varied age groups. The young career-minded, age 25 to 40 who, in planning for retirement (and it is never too soon, as illustrated in various charts earlier in this book), should be aggressive for the long term; the mid-productive years of 40 to 50, followed by the pre-retirement years of 50 to 60; and ultimately the retirement years of 60 and up.

Reviewing these choices may help you decide just how aggressive or conservative you want to be. Note that I am indicating cycles of 10 or more years. As previously stated, long-term investing overcomes the effect of market volatility cycles. It gives you time to chart the progress of your portfolio and to make occasional, well-planned changes. Unless you want to become a "market timer," which is not encouraged here due to higher risks involved, stick with buy-and-hold for long term. We will deal with market timing, dollar cost averaging, and value averaging in Chapter 9, where we will discuss the occasional changes you may wish to make and the reasons.

THE 401(k) PLAN

Since over 45 million American employees are now eligible for this plan, it deserves sufficient explanation in this chapter to help those who can take advantage of it before discussing portfolio construction.

The 401(k) is a plan in which you, the employee, can make contributions of pre-tax dollars to an investment account which will compound tax free until you withdraw part or all of it. You may also hear this called the salary reduction plan.

Because you can choose where your money is invested, you now become your own pension fund manager. This is a substantial responsibility, especially for those who have no investment experience.

You have already discovered what just $1,000 can grow to when compounded for 25, 30, or 35 years. The 401(k) is really a revolution in finance. Most employers will let you borrow from your plan, and if you have an emergency of a serious nature you can withdraw funds without penalty.

Since a majority of 401(k) plans give you the opportunity to choose from multiple investments, you have the chance to diversify your investment and to seek maximum growth by the time you are ready for retirement.

If you are young when starting your 401(k), do not make the mistake of investing in guaranteed investment contracts or other interest-paying investments. Over the long term, inflation will devour most of your earnings. You have the time to ride out the volatility of the market by investing in stock funds, and you are doing so by dollar cost averaging which decreases the volatility, as you will find in Chapter 9, on strategies.

Many 401(k) plans offer the opportunity to invest in the stock of the company where you are employed. I strongly recommend that you leave company stock out of your plan. Your attachment to your employer plays on your emotions, and you may find you are reluctant to sell that stock if it is doing poorly in the market place.

Do not make the mistake of investing only in money market funds. With the rise and fall of interest rates, you cannot keep ahead of inflation with just interest-bearing investments. *A point of interest:* If you are old enough to have been alive in 1926 and had invested $1,000 in common stocks and another $1,000 in long-term treasury bonds, your stocks by 1990 would be worth approximately half a million dollars. Your treasury bonds would be worth between $20,000 and $21,000.

Diversification, however, is important. For young individuals, I recommend placing 70 percent or more of your money in aggressive growth or long-term growth funds and the remainder in balanced funds and intermediate-term bond funds, where you will get growth as well as interest. As you get older, you can gradually reverse these percentages. The following will give you many ideas on how to create diversified portfolios at different ages.

INVESTOR PROFILES

Following are basics or general profiles of investors which led to the creation of these portfolios. Obviously, the description does not necessarily fit every investor in the category, so your own adjustments to your particular circumstances should be taken into consideration.

—*Ages 25 to 40—young career minded:* Lower monthly income during this period would be one of the reasons for the emergency money market account. You do not need income from your investments at this time. You will not, normally, need liquidity, but you will always have it with no-load mutual funds. Your tax bracket during this period will normally be low. Your tolerance for risk should be high, and you are investing for the long term.

In the portfolio construction section you will note that international stock funds, aggressive growth, and long-term growth funds during this period, as well as a money market fund are recommended. The aggressive funds should include small capital or emerging growth funds, as well as aggressive funds, investing in older growth industries.

—Ages 40 to 50—mid-productive years: In this category a choice of five portfolios are illustrated. One continues the aggressive group in the 25 to 40 age group. The balance include moderate portfolios which increase the amount of liquid assets in the money market account and reduces the aggressive and long-term growth categories for less volatility. Lastly, conservative portfolios for this period increase the money market portion and reduce equity fund holdings.

Do not watch these fund portfolios too often as they will, in the short term, show more volatility, but in the long term they will achieve the capital accumulation for your retirement.

—Ages 50 to 60—pre-retirement years: This portfolio begins to move to a more conservative approach, bond funds are added and the percentage of aggressive growth funds is reduced. There are two portfolios in this category—moderate and conservative.

—Ages 60 and up—the retirement years: This group has two portfolios—a conservative portfolio and a very conser-

vative portfolio. However, even in retirement, a portion of the portfolio should be in growth funds in order to protect against inflation and the erosion of buying power.

Investors in this last profile should consider a good aggressive growth fund which may invest only in stocks which have paid dividends for long periods. These dividends can then be either reinvested if income is not needed, or if income is needed, a check as dividends are declared can be received. If you are now in a high tax bracket, and this would apply to ages 50 to 60 as well, you may wish to invest in tax-free bond funds, rather than taxable bond funds where indicated in the individual portfolios that follow.

CONSTRUCTING YOUR PERSONAL INVESTMENT PORTFOLIO

The make-up of the following portfolios has been based on long-term investing and reinvesting dividends (except in the retirement portfolios where you may want them sent to you for income) in order to compound your growth as rapidly as possible. Once again, you should establish a separate money market account with three to six months' income so as not to disturb or interrupt the progress of your portfolio. Most portfolios will indicate money market funds as part of the portfolio, not the emergency reserve money market account.

Special note: If you invest in more than one fund family, you may want to divide the money market percentage so that you will have a money market fund with each family in which you are invested.

Portfolios for ages 25 (or younger) to 40

Very aggressive portfolio

30% in 3 sector funds
20% in 1 capital appreciation fund
20% in 1 small capital fund
10% in 1 long-term growth fund
10% in 1 global fund
10% in 1 money market fund

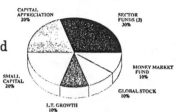

Aggressive long-term portfolio

15% in 1 income fund
15% in 1 high yield bond fund
15% in 1 small capital fund
35% in 2 long-term growth funds
20% in 2 aggressive growth funds

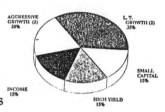

Moderately aggressive portfolio

10% in 1 capital appreciation fund
10% in 1 small capital fund
10% in 1 international stock fund
10% in 1 global equity fund
20% in 2 long-term growth funds
15% in 1 balanced fund
15% in 1 equity-income fund
10% in 1 money market fund

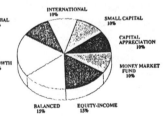

Portfolios for ages 40 to 50

Aggressive portfolio
(Continue Portfolio for ages 25-40.)

Less aggressive portfolio

35% in 2 aggressive growth funds
35% in 2 long-term growth funds
10% in 1 international stock fund
20% in 1 money market fund

Moderately aggressive portfolio

30% in 2 aggressive growth funds
30% in 2 long-term growth funds
10% in 1 international stock fund
30% in 2 money market funds

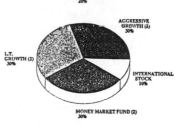

Moderate portfolio

15% in 1 aggressive growth fund
15% in 1 international stock fund
15% in 1 growth-income fund
15% in 1 income fund
20% in 2 bond funds (consider tax-free)
20% in 2 money market funds

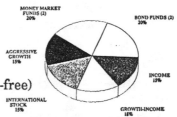

Conservative portfolio

10% in 1 aggressive growth fund
20% in 2 long-term growth funds
10% in 1 international bond fund
10% in 1 international stock fund
15% in 1 balanced fund
15% in 1 equity income fund
20% in 2 money market funds *OR*
10% in 1 sector fund & 10% in 1 money market fund

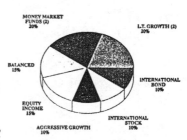

Portfolios for ages 50 to 60

Moderate portfolio

10% in 1 international bond fund
10% in 1 aggressive growth fund
15% in 1 growth-income fund
15% in 1 balanced fund
30% in 2 bond funds (consider tax-free)
20% in 2 money market funds

Conservative portfolio

20% in 1 govt bond or treasury fund
20% in 1 invstmnt grd corp bond fund
10% in 1 balanced fund
10% in 1 growth-income fund
10% in 1 long-term growth fund
10% in 1 international bond fund
20% in 2 money market funds

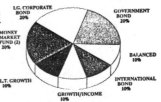

Portfolios for retirement ages 60 and up

Conservative portfolio

10% in 1 long-term growth fund
10% in 1 international bond fund
30% in 3 income funds
20% in 1 tax-free bond fund
15% in 1 govt or treasury fund
15% in 1 money market fund

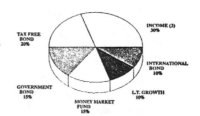

Very conservative portfolio

10% in 1 growth-income fund
10% in 1 income fund
10% in 1 international bond fund
10% in 1 govt or treasury fund
10% in 1 balanced fund
40% in 2 money market funds
10% in 1 investment grade corporate bond fund

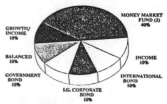

Remember that if you are too conservative and invest too much in bond funds, you can cause the erosion of principal due to inflation. Table 8-1 illustrates this point.

A word of caution: As you approach that period when you will be switching from the more aggressive portfolio to the conservative funds desired in your retirement years, these changes should be very gradual and not sudden in order to avoid making sudden moves into changing markets. For example, if you are looking ahead to the type of portfolio presented here for ages 60 and up and you have been aggressively investing toward your retirement goal, you should begin switching two to three years before and moving your aggressive funds just 20 to 25 percent at a time, every three to four months, into one of the recommended funds in the retirement portfolio. Perhaps a bond fund or a balanced fund would be good. In other words, use dollar cost averaging, discussed in the next chapter, to make your changes.

Again, in looking at these portfolio suggestions, you need not accept them to the letter. Make substitutions and adjustments to meet your objectives.

You should watch the *aggressive* and *very aggressive* portfolios closely and possibly, when the market appears to turn bearish and you think it may be bearish for a long period, there are defensive actions you can take which will be discussed in Chapter 9.

A FEW REMINDERS

Try to select funds with good records during bear markets. These are the ones which will likely show much less volatility and keep a steady pace in growth.

Avoid high expenses. Invest in no-load funds, avoid loads, 12b-1 fees, redemption fees, a contingent deferred sales charge (a sliding scale of fees usually over a 7-year period, if you sell any time during the first seven years).

TABLE 8-1: IMPACT OF 5% INFLATION ON PRINCIPAL $100,000 BOND

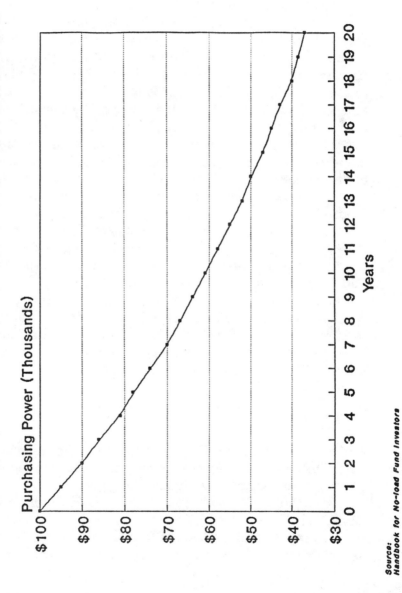

Source:
Handbook for No-Load Fund Investors

Be sure to read and understand the prospectus. Look for dividend reinvestment fees and exchange fees charged when you wish to switch one fund for another in the same fund family. You should avoid these funds.

Remember, all funds, load and no-load, have management fees and expenses, but there is no reason to incur more than the following averages:

- stock funds 1.2 percent

- fixed income (bond funds) less than 1 percent

The total expenses of a fund company include the commissions paid when purchasing stocks or bonds, costs of printing, administration, management fees, and the other expenses of business operations.

Strategies in Mutual Fund Investing

There are several investment strategies you can use with mutual funds. These range from the simple dollar cost averaging strategy to the more complex market timing strategies using technical indicators. Following is a brief discussion on the most popular including the new variation to dollar cost averaging called value averaging.

DOLLAR COST AVERAGING

This is the simplest of all strategies and consists of investing a set amount at very regular intervals, such as $100 per month. It is especially effective for long-term investing which, of course, has been emphasized throughout this book.

Dollar cost averaging works much better with no-load funds than with any other investment. You can keep adding to your investment without commissions. If you invest in stocks using dollar cost averaging, your investments would be eroded by brokerage commissions.

Through dollar cost averaging, the volatility of your investment is reduced because the risk of investing heavily at a peak is avoided and the loss factor during drops in the fund price is avoided. With dollar cost averaging you invest the same amount regardless of the rise and fall of the market. Remember, you do not have an actual loss or profit in your fund(s) unless you make a sale. When the fund drops you will be buying more shares, and when it rises you will be buying fewer.

Even when you have a lump sum to invest, put that amount into a money market fund in the fund family you select and then, on a regular basis, dollar average through telephone switching to the fund you select. Believe it or not, you will reap greater profit with the market fluctuation than if the market goes steadily up without a decline.

In Figure 9-1 there are four graphs indicating the results of dollar averaging under different circumstances.

Each graph starts with investing $100 per month for seven months with the original price per share at $10. In order for dollar cost averaging to work, it is important to stick with your investment regularity. Do not stop if the market turns down; you will defeat the entire purpose of dollar cost averaging.

Dollar cost averaging is not practical for large sums of money, such as $100,000 or more. Averaging such sums over a 24-month period, for example, could result in missing a good bull market. When investing a lump sum of money, it is better to decide on a portfolio with diversification, such as the examples in Chapter 8, and invest for the long term.

A word of caution. When investing a particularly large sum of money, check with the fund customer service representative to determine whether a dividend is to be declared in the next 30 days. If so, and you proceed to invest, you will incur a tax on the dividend. Inasmuch as the NAV of a fund drops by the amount of the dividend, you will, of course, receive more shares, but if you wait until after the dividend to invest, you will avoid the tax and pick up the fund at a lower price. This is particularly important prior to a capital gain dividend, usually paid by most funds in December.

FIGURE 9-1: RESULTS OF DOLLAR COST AVERAGING

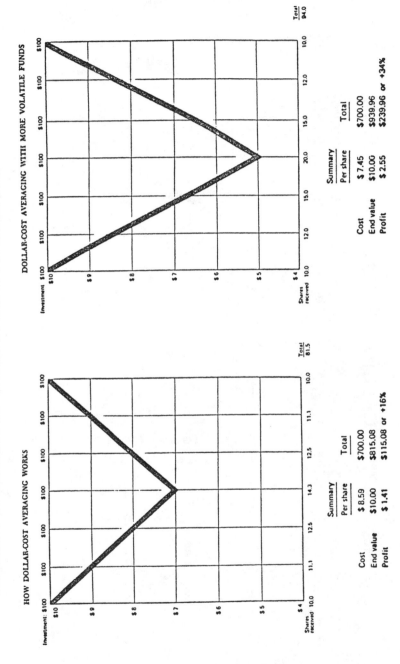

FIGURE 9-1: RESULTS OF DOLLAR COST AVERAGING, Continued

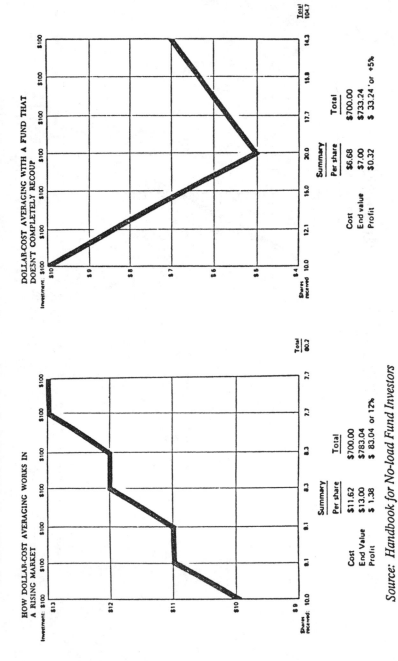

Source: Handbook for No-load Fund Investors

With tax-sheltered plans such as an IRA, Keogh, 401(k), you are already into dollar cost averaging, and you should put away as much as possible, as regularly as possible. Dividends on your tax-sheltered plans are not taxable, nor can you take tax deductions on losses.

VALUE AVERAGING

Value averaging is a variation of dollar cost averaging. The main difference is that rather than investing a fixed amount each month, you make the value of your investment grow by a *predetermined* amount each month or other period of time. For instance, if you use the dollar cost averaging strategy and invest $100 per month for a year, at the end of the 12-month period you would have invested $1,200. However, due to per-share price fluctuations, you would have bought more shares when prices were low and fewer shares when prices were high making the value of your investment fluctuate at the same level.

With value averaging, you would first determine the amount you would like your investment to grow over each period. Then you would adjust the number of shares you purchased based on this predetermined amount. For example, say you wanted your investment to grow by $100 dollars a month. If, in the first month of your investment program the share price of your no-load fund was $4.64, then you would buy 21.55 shares. If, in the second month, the share price dropped to $4.38 you would purchase 24.11 shares to make the value of your investment grow to $200. $200 divided by $4.38 results in a total of 45.66 shares you need to own. Since in month one you purchased 21.55 shares, you only need to purchase 24.11 shares at $4.38 to make the value $200.

Table 9-1 shows an example of the value averaging strategy. If you look under the "share price" and "amount invested" columns, you will see that when the share price goes down, you will have to spend more than $100 in order to replace the lost value. However, also note that when share price goes up, you will have to spend less than $100, since the increased price has already given you the necessary increase in the value of your investment.

The value averaging strategy also calls for selling shares when there is a large upward price swing. For instance, in Table 9-1, the eighth month shows that the price increased enough to increase the value of the fund over the predetermined amount for that month; in fact, it is $42.81 over. When this happens, the VA strategy tells you to sell $42.81 worth of shares—11.89. But, since you want to avoid any capital gain or loss, with possible tax liability—these costs will lower your return—I suggest you simply hold on to your extra shares and don't sell. Wait until the strategy tells you it's time to buy more shares.

Value averaging works well with no-load mutual funds that allow telephone switching between their money market fund—where you have your pre-planned holding—and the fund you are investing in. This strategy is useful for anyone who needs to accumulate a certain sum—say, $30,000 for college—over a long period of time.

Here are a few *don't*s you should remember for both the dollar cost averaging and value averaging strategies:

- Don't use value averaging instead of dollar cost averaging if it will result in costly transactions fees.

- Don't use value averaging unless you plan to monitor your investment at least each quarter; dollar cost averaging is automatic;

- Don't "spend your winnings" when you sell shares using value averaging. You will need them for the

TABLE 9-1: VALUE AVERAGING: AN EXAMPLE

Month*	Share Price ($)	Total Value ($)	No. of Shares To Own	Total No. of Shares To Buy	Amount Invested ($)
			Value Averaging		
1	4.64	100	21.55	21.55	100.00
2	4.38	200	45.66	24.11	105.60
3	4.56	300	65.79	20.13	91.78
4	4.25	400	94.12	28.33	120.39
5	3.81	500	131.23	37.12	141.41
6	3.19	600	188.09	56.85	181.36
7	2.99	700	234.11	46.03	137.62
8	3.60	800	222.22	-11.89	-42.81
9	4.70	900	191.49	-30.73	-144.44
10	4.41	1,000	226.76	35.27	155.53
11	4.34	1,100	253.46	26.70	115.87
12	4.69	1,200	255.86	2.41	11.29
1	5.26	1,300	247.15	-8.72	-45.84
2	4.54	1,400	308.37	61.22	277.95
3	5.38	1,500	278.81	-29.56	-156.03
4	7.47	1,600	214.19	-64.62	-482.71
5	7.39	1,700	230.04	15.85	117.14
6	6.31	1,800	285.26	55.22	348.44
7	7.07	1,900	268.74	-16.52	-116.80
8	6.48	2,000	308.64	39.90	258.56
9	7.07	2,100	297.03	-11.61	-82.10
10	6.96	2,200	316.09	19.06	132.67
11	5.05	2,300	455.45	139.35	703.74
12	5.80	2,400	413.79	-41.65	-241.58
1	5.06	-	-	-	-

Ave. Share Price $5.18

Total Invested $1,684.00
Final Value $2,094.00

*Beginning of Month

next period when you must buy a larger amount of shares; and

- Don't make any purchase or sale that you are not comfortable with. It's your investment!

PRE-DIVIDEND SWITCHING

Some investors believe that they should sell or switch a fund just before a dividend date, thinking they can buy it back at a lower price after the dividend. This would be considered a "wash sale," and the results are as follows:

- If you had a loss in selling or switching the fund, you may not take a tax deduction.

- If you had a gain when you switched, you would pay tax on the gain.

A note of caution. If you are tempted to use this strategy to gain back a loss by switching out just before the dividend and switching back in at the lower price and still claim your loss, you must wait until 31 days following your sale or switch before you can buy back.

MARKET TIMING

There are many investors who "time" the market. If a market timer believes the market is going to take a substantial drop in value, they will switch some or all of the funds to money market accounts and reinvest when they believe the market has "bottomed."

Timing the market takes close watch of technical indications such as interest rate trends, P/E ratios, dividend averages, book value ratios, and insider trading activities. And even a close watch does not guarantee results.

There are financial newsletter writers who advise when to buy and when to sell. Probably the simplest method is charting moving averages while keeping track of the net asset value (NAV) of the fund. The strategy works like this: When the NAV moves above the fund's moving average, shares are bought; when the NAV goes below the moving average, shares are sold if the trend is downward.

There are also money managers who specialize in market timing and will manage your funds for you. However, 75 percent of the time the market will be moving up, and by using the buy and hold strategy suggested in this book you will be correct three-fourths of the time.

Here's a case in point. If you had selected the poorest day in the year when the price of funds were at their peak during the 20-year period 1969 through 1988 and invested $2,000 per year in the S&P 500 index, you would have been a big winner. You would have invested a total of $40,000, and your gain by the end of 1988 would have been $130,000, or an average of slightly over 10 percent per year.

There are some market timers who might be correct more than three-fourths of the time, but it is possible they could be wrong more than 25 percent of the time.

Remember, any profit you make when you switch is subject to a capital gains tax. Also, market timing signals can be wrong. You can be *whipsawed* if you switch out of your fund on a down signal and the market quickly recovers and starts back up. To get back into your fund will now cost more than the price you sold it for.

A great deal of pro and con opinion on market timing exists and, if it is of interest to you, a number of good, well-written books on mutual funds and market timing with considerably more technical information are available at your public library.

DEFENSIVE FUNDING

Rather than switch to money market funds with market timing, there is a middle-of-the-road approach called "defensive" funding. You will probably want to make a switch in funds occasionally since very few funds are consistently good in both up and down markets. When the market is on the rise, you will want to be in aggressive funds (except in retirement, unless you have excess cash with which you can take some risk).

When the market appears to be heading downward, you will want to be in more conservative funds. Remaining fully invested is desirable, but not necessarily at all times in an aggressive or a conservative posture. By switching in this manner, you will have given yourself reasonable downside protection by being defensive. As mentioned above, if you time the market or have a market timer do it for you, there is the risk of a whipsaw. By using the defensive funding strategy, you can eliminate this risk. Also, if you use dollar cost averaging to make these switches it will be advantageous, since it is rare that anyone sells at the actual top or buys at the very bottom.

THE AGGRESSIVE TO CONSERVATIVE SWITCH FORMULA

There is a formula which has proven very helpful in indicating when to be in aggressive funds and when to be in conservative funds. The formula is simple but, again, there are no guarantees that it will always work.

In *Barron's*, the financial newspaper which is published every Saturday, you will find the yields for the S&P 500 stocks. By dividing the numeral 1 by the yield you can determine the price/dividend ratio. For example: a 4.2 percent yield translates into a price/dividend ratio of 24. A 3.5 percent yield translates into a price/dividend ratios of 29. Determining the average of all the price/dividend ratios will give you an indication of the action to take. The guidelines are as follows: If the price/dividend ratio average is above 30, the market is at a peak, and you should become conservative. If the price/dividend ratio average decline is below 20, you should become very aggressive.

Tables 9-2A and 9-2B serve as a guide on how to allocate your portfolio at various levels of price/dividend ratios.

TABLE 9-2A: ALLOCATIONS WHILE STAYING FULLY INVESTED

P/D Ratio	Conservative Funds	Aggressive Funds
34+	100.0%	0.0%
30-34	87.5%	12.5%
23-30	62.5%	37.5%
20-23	37.5%	62.5%
-20	0.0%	100.0%

TABLE 9-2B: ALLOCATIONS INCLUDING CASH

P/D Ratio	Money Funds	Conservative Funds	Aggressive Funds
34+	50.0%	50.0%	0.0%
32-34	15.0%	75.0%	10.0%
30-23	10.0%	55.0%	35.0%
23-30	0.0%	50.0%	50.0%
20-23	0.0%	37.5%	62.5%
-20	0.0%	0.0%	100.0%

Source: *Handbook for No-Load Fund Investors*

SYSTEMATIC WITHDRAWAL PROGRAMS IN RETIREMENT

In the prologue I mentioned a systematic withdrawal program to obtain monthly income for my mother's needs and still preserve her capital. I still use the same format now with financial planning.

In Chapter 8 I cautioned against being too conservative in your investments, pointing out the erosion of principal which can take place with inflation. This can be avoided, even in the most conservative portfolio by selecting a growth and income fund, an income fund, and a balanced fund. All will provide both growth and some income.

Carefully selected funds in these categories should average a total return of 12 percent to 14 percent per year. You can arrange to have the fund company in each case send you a monthly check based on a withdrawal of 8 percent per year. As long as you do not suddenly decide to withdraw a large sum of money, your fund will continue to grow faster than the amount of withdrawal, thus preserving your principal.

This will also keep your taxes lower. For example: if you invest $50,000 in a growth and income fund, growing at a rate of 12 percent per year and you draw $300 per month, the fund sells a few of your shares each month to send you the amount you have requested. Assume that you bought your shares at $10 per share and at the end of the first month your shares have increased in value to $11. The fund will then sell 27.273 (300 divided by 11) shares to provide you with $300. You have earned $1 per share on 27.273 shares. You will only be taxed on $27.27. The other $272.73 is return of principal. Your $50,000 purchased 5,000 shares of the fund. You now have 4,972.728 shares left which are worth, at $11 per share, $54,700.

Assume that the market had a poor year and your fund only grew by 7 percent and you need to draw 9 percent. You could continue to draw 9 percent per year and it would take 22 years before your money would be depleted. However, it is highly unlikely that such circumstances would last more than 18 to 24 months in a bear market. Remember that the market is up 75 percent of the time, and if you have a good steady fund in the categories mentioned you should do very well by drawing up to 8 percent or 9 percent of your investment per year from a fund whose 5 to 10 year history shows an average return of 12 to 14 percent per year.

OTHER STRATEGIES

There are several other, sometimes complicated, strategies used by sophisticated market timers: seasonal indicators; interest rate effects, which base decisions of buying and selling on treasury bill rates of interest; another based on prime rates; and another based on federal discount rates. These strategies are all in the category of market timing, which requires constant monitoring of your portfolio of funds. The buy and hold technique, remaining constantly invested over the long period and using the defensive funding approach during volatile or down periods is suggested. This allows you to reallocate your more aggressive positions to conservative positions while riding out the volatility.

More details on the highly sophisticated techniques can be found in many books available at your library or bookstore.

Questions and Answers

This chapter contains questions frequently asked by the beginning mutual fund investor. Following each question is a general answer. If a topic has been covered more thoroughly earlier, I have directed you to those chapters.

Q: Is it advisable to include international mutual funds in my portfolio?

A: Yes. The economy is going more and more global, and you should have at least one good global or international fund. No-load, of course. International funds invest only in overseas securities. Global funds invest in overseas and some United States securities. There are equity funds, as well as bond funds, in each.

Q: I have been investing in CDs, treasuries, and bonds. With interest rates dropping so much, where do I place these as they mature?

A: Stop chasing yields. Be more aggressive, especially if you are willing to invest long term. See the portfolio recommendations in Chapter 8 and select a portfolio compatible with your age. If you are bent on being conservative and have carefully considered the effect of inflation on your investment return, then you should invest in one international bond fund, one high yield bond fund, and one long-term high quality corporate bond fund to obtain a high average return.

Q: Taking fund families as a whole, is it true that no-load funds have proven to give better performance than load funds?

A: Yes, no-load fund families, according to an analysis of 8 such families versus 22 load fund families found the following results:

	Total Return
No-load fund families	94%
S&P 500 Index	93%
Load fund families	88%

You get absolutely nothing extra by investing in a load fund except to make a salesperson happy and richer with your money.

Q: What are the most frequent mistakes people make when investing for retirement?

A: The best answer I can give you for that is to quote Bill Donoghue of the *Donoghue Money Letter*. I happen to agree with Bill who writes as follows:

Your retirement years can easily account for 25-33 percent of your adult life. Controlling your own financial destiny can be a rich, rewarding and most satisfying experience when you are ready to retire. Additional numbers of senior citizens are joining the growing ranks of those doing their own investing. The important thing is to avoid disaster with too many missteps and to help you avoid this, I have listed the ten largest mistakes which retired investors are making.

Mistake #1: Investing for income instead of cash flow. Retired investors too often think of generating enough income to replace their customary paycheck. In reality, all they need is just enough cash to pay the monthly bills. The rest should be devoted to growth investments to shelter savings from inflation.

Mistake #2: Investing your IRA, or other tax deferred money, too conservatively. You should actually invest IRA money more aggressively then other funds. In an IRA, all the money you would have paid in taxes is being reinvested in new investments every time you receive a distribution or take profits.

Mistake #3: Letting a commissioned salesperson make your investment decisions. You would not completely trust a car salesperson when buying a car, so why trust a larger and more important purchase to a stockbroker?

Mistake #4: Trusting a banker to advise you on investments. No one ever took a test to be a banker. There are no minimum education or licensing requirements.

Mistake #5: Investing in something you do not understand. Take time to learn about investment alternatives. Jumping on the first good story you are told (or sold) can cost you a comfortable retirement.

Mistake #6: Underestimating your own investment skills. Too many people work hard to save enough money for their retirement then let it dribble away because they do not trust their own judgement.

Mistake #7: *Not understanding your rights as an investor. If you feel you have been ripped off, write your story down. Discuss it with your state securities administrator or call the North American Securities Administrators Association in Washington for advice and referrals.*

Mistake #8: *Letting tax considerations rule your investment decisions. Other than avoiding the fifty percent (50%) tax penalty on IRA withdrawals, you should always put more emphasis on the after-tax benefits of your investments, rather than just investing to avoid taxes.*

Mistake #9: *Drawing your IRA too slowly. Get Publication #590 from the International Revenue Service and make sure you are withdrawing the correct amount from your IRA each and every year to avoid the fifty percent (50%) tax penalty.*

Mistake #10: *Drawing your IRA too quickly. If you have a choice, draw down only the minimum amount from your IRA and let the rest continue compounding on a pretax basis. This way you get the maximum bang per buck from your IRA.*

Q: You seem to discourage market timing for the average investor. How difficult is it to "time the market"? What are the best indicators?

A: Timing the market is difficult, even for the most professional and no one does a perfect job. Following are the influencing factors which need to be considered in timing the market:

MARKET INFLUENCES—MARKET TIMING TECHNIQUES

Fundamental Factors	*Technical Factors*	*Sentiment Indicators*
Unemployment	Advances to	Short Sales
World News and	Decline Ratios	Corporate Insider
Events	Price/Earnings	Trading
GNP	Ratio	Odd Lot Trading
Productivity	Dow Jones	Credit Card Debt
Interest Rates	Industrial	Mutual Fund
Inflation	Momentum	Cash on Hand
Money Supply	Volumes	Retail Sales
Recession	Moving Averages	
	Price/Dividend	
	Ratios	

About Newsletters and Other Information Sources

NEWSLETTERS

Unlike newsletters which give information on stocks, bonds, and the general market, there are about 25 newsletters devoted to the long-term investor in mutual funds. Rather than giving tips on stock movements, these letter writers encourage long-term investing in mutual funds. Many provide advice through model portfolios for different investor profiles—conservative, moderate, and aggressive. In addition, most mutual fund letter writers follow large numbers of funds, mostly no-load, and give their recommendations for buy, hold, or sell.

Mutual fund letter writers can be divided into two categories: those who give advice on market timing and those who recommend asset allocation. The latter are likely to have model portfolios. They offer you suggestions on percentages to keep in equity funds, bond funds, and money market funds.

The market timing letters may also offer portfolios and, additionally, advise on when to be in-or-out-of-the-market. Both asset allocation and market timing were discussed in earlier chapters.

Newsletter writers give their personal opinions on the market direction and the economy in general. The letters make interesting reading and, whether right or wrong, they may be of some help in forming your own opinion.

Most of the mutual fund letters keep you informed of the day to day "behind the scenes" activities in the fund families, including changes, new funds, new managers, and other important data.

You can obtain a free sample of most newsletters. You should get and read as many as possible, determine which one or two best suit your objectives, and then subscribe to one or two. The cost of annual subscriptions runs from $99 to $179.

A word of caution. These advisers are human. They make mistakes just as you and I do. No one can foretell the future. One newsletter tracks over 125 newsletters recording their successes and their failures and ranks them. Those who were in the top ten last year could be at the bottom this year. A very small percentage of newsletter writers manage to maintain a steady record of success.

The following list includes some of the more popular newsletter sources. There are, of course, other sources at your library and neighborhood bookstore.

BOOKS AND PERIODICALS

Barron's (Saturday only), *Forbes, Money* magazine and the *Wall Street Journal.* Available at your news dealer.

Books: *The Donoghue Strategies,* by William Donoghue; *The Fidelity Guide to Mutual Funds,* by M. Rowland; *The Handbook For No-Load Fund Investors,* by Sheldon Jacobs; *Individual Investor's Guide to No-load Mutual Funds,* by American Association of Individual Investors, International Publishing Corporation; *Mutual Funds—How to Invest With the Pros,* by K. Brouwer.

I discussed earlier various aspects of mutual fund newsletter writers, their advice and model portfolios. I also mentioned one newsletter which tracks the successes and failures of 130 newsletters. In order to determine which newsletters have been most successful from the standpoint of model portfolios investors might want to subscribe to:

Hulbert Financial Digest, editor, Mark Hulbert
316 Commerce Street
Alexandria, VA 22314 703/683-5905

For my own purposes, I like the following newsletters for updated information as well as portfolio recommendations:

5-Star Investor
Morningstar Inc.
53 Jackson Street
Chicago, IL 60604
1-800/876-5005

No-Load Fund Investor
Editor Sheldon Jacobs
P.O. Box 283
Hastings-on-Hudson,
  NY 10706
1-800/252-2042

No-Load Fund X
Editor Burt Berry
235 Montgomery Street
San Francisco, CA 94104
415/986-7979

Mutual Fund Investing
Editor Jay Schabacker
15245 Shady Grove
Rockville, MD 20850
1-800/346-6138

For very helpful informative letters I also read:

Louis Rukeyser's Wall Street
1101 King Street, Suite 400
Alexandria, VA 22314

Mutual Fundamentals
Editor Don McDonald
Colorado Springs, CO
  80933
719/634-1414

There are several others which are also very good and, of course, those with which I have no experience I cannot judge but the facts are available in the *Hulbert Financial Digest.*

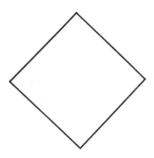

Appendix I: No-Load Mutual Fund Families

The following no-load mutual fund families are selected on the basis of having sufficient funds to provide a good asset allocation program. By obtaining a prospectus on each fund which is of interest, you can develop a diversified portfolio in a single family of funds if you wish. However, before choosing any one fund it is wise to compare that fund's record with other funds in the same category with the same objectives. There are, of course, many other true no-load mutual funds from which to make a selection. You need only look at the mutual fund page of most metropolitan newspapers or the Saturday issue of *Barron's* or the *Wall Street Journal* to find out other small fund families or individual no-load funds. How to identify true no-load mutual funds is described in Chapter 2.

AARP FUNDS
160 Federal Street
Boston, MA 02110
1-800/253-2277

BABSON FUNDS
3 Crown Center
2440 Pershing Road
Kansas City, MO 64108
1-800/422-4766

BENHAM FUNDS
1665 Charleston Road
Mountain View, CA 94043
1-800/321-8321

DIMENSIONAL FUNDS
(DFA)
1299 Ocean Ave, Suite 650
Santa Monica, CA 90401
1-213/395-8005

EVERGREEN FUNDS
2500 Westchester Avenue
Purchase, NY 10577
1-800/235-0064

FEDERATED FUNDS
Federated Investor Tower
Pittsburgh, PA 15222-3779
1-800/245-5000 or -5040

FINANCIAL FUNDS
(INVESCO)
7800 E. Union Avenue
Denver, CO 80237
1-800/525-8085
1-303/779-1233

HARBOR FUNDS
One SeaGate
Toledo, OH 43666
1-800/422-1050

JANUS FUNDS
100 Fillmore Street
Denver, CO 80206
1-800/525-3713

LEXINGTON FUNDS
P.O. Box 1515
Park 80 West Plaza 2
Saddle Brook, NJ 07662
1-800/526-0056

MERRIMAN FUNDS
(Market Timed)
1200 Westlake Avenue N.
Seattle, WA 98109-3530
1-800/423-4893

NEUBERGER & BERMAN
342 Madison Avenue
New York, NY 10173
1-800/877-9700

T. ROWE PRICE FUNDS
100 E. Pratt
Baltimore, MD 21202
Ph: 1/800/638-5660

RUSHMORE FUNDS
4922 Fairmont Avenue
Bethesda, MD 20814
1-800/343-3355

SAFECO FUNDS
P.O. Box 34890
Seattle, WA 98124-1890
1-800/426-6730

SCUDDER FUNDS
160 Federal Street
Boston, MA 02110
1-800/225-5163

STEIN ROE FUNDS
300 W. Adams
Chicago, IL 60606
1-880/338-2550

STRONG FUNDS
100 Heritage Reserve
P.O. Box 2936
Milwaukee, WI 53201
1-800/368-3863

TWENTIETH CENTURY
4500 Main Street
Kansas City, MO 64111
1-800/345-2021

UNITED SERVICES FUNDS
P.O. Box 29467
San Antonio, TX 78229-0467
1-800/873-8637

USAA FUNDS
USAA Building
San Antonio, TX 78288
1-800/531-8181/8448

VALUE LINE FUNDS
711 Third Avenue
New York, NY 10017
1-800/223-0818

VANGUARD FUNDS
P.O. Box 2600
Valley Forge, PA 19482
1-800/662-2739/7447

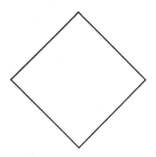

Appendix II: Mutual Fund Record and Rating Sheets

MUTUAL FUND RECORDKEEPING SYSTEM

Recordkeeping of your mutual fund purchases and redemptions can be accomplished very easily by using the record sheets found on page 117.

In order to determine gain or loss on your redemptions, it is easiest to use the average cost when you have maintained a fund for a long period with a number of entries. To determine average cost add up your total dollar purchases in Column 4; then add up the total number of shares purchases in Column 2. Divide the total dollars by the total shares purchased and the answer is your average cost per share.

Whenever you make a redemption, enter the average cost in Column 7 on the same line with the selling price (Column 8). If the sell price is larger, subtract the average cost. This will give you the amount of profit per share. Multiply this figure by the number of shares sold (Column 5) to determine your gain. Enter this figure in Column 10 with a plus (+) sign to show gain.

If your selling price is less than your average cost, then subtract the selling price from the average cost to determine your loss per share. Multiply the loss per share by the number of shares sold in Column 5. The answer is your total loss and should be entered in Column 10 in Bracket ( ) to indicate loss. You will receive statement on your accounts from your mutual fund company whenever there are transactions, not necessary every month. Each statement will list all transactions for the year-to-date. Therefore, it is not necessary to keep the old statement once you determine that the new statement has all the transactions to date. Dispose of the old statement and keep the new along with your own mutual fund record sheet.

At the end of the year, you should have only the two sheets in your notebook for each fund you own.

MUTUAL FUND RATING SHEET

Starting on page 118 is the mutual fund rating sheet showing all the factors you should consider before deciding on a fund. Each factor is explained at the end of the listing. Basically, in the long term—five years or more—most mutual funds become low-risk. To lose your principal altogether is highly unlikely. It would take a worldwide economic collapse for such a thing to happen. Your fund has such a large portfolio of stocks or bonds that it would be impossible for 50 to 100 securities to become worthless all at one time.

The risk of volatility is, of course, always present but look at the beta rating of each fund to determine the probable volatility. (See Appendix III for definitions of some terms not mentioned earlier in the body of the book.)

MUTUAL FUND RECORD SHEET

Fund Name: _____

Address: _____

City/State/Zip: _____

Phone: _____ Account #: _____

PURCHASES INCLUDING DIVIDENDS				REDEMPTION INFORMATION					
1. Date	2. No. of Shares	3. Share Price ($)	4. Total ($)	5. No. Shares Sold	6. Share Balance	7. Average Cost/Share	8. Sell Price	9. Totals ($)	10. Gain/Loss +(-)
TOTAL -->		TOTAL -->							

MUTUAL FUND RATING SHEET

Date of Report: _____

Name of Fund: _____

Where Located: _____

_____

Type of Fund: _____

NAV: _____

Sharpe Performance Rating: _____

Sharpe Rank Rating: _____

Risk: _____

Treynor Performance Rating: _____

Treynor Rank Rating: _____

Alpha: _____

Beta: _____

Diversification Index: _____

Correlation Coefficient: _____

Front-end Sales Load: _____

Deferred Sales Charge: _____

Redemption: _____

Management Fee (per year): _____

Portfolio Assets: _____

Cash (%): _____

Turnover (Annual): _____

Minimum Purchase: _____

Subsequent Purchase: _____

Value of $1,000 after 3 years: _____

Value of $1,000 after 5 years: _____

Value of $1,000 after 10 years: _____

Beginning Date of Fund: _____

Last Month Performance: _____

GAIN OR LOSS:
3 Months: _____

6 Months: _____

Latest 12 Months: _____

GAIN OR LOSS:
Year-to-date: _____

Dividend Yield: _____

YEARLY TOTAL RETURN (10 Years or Since Inception)

1991   _____

1990   _____

1989   _____

1988   _____

1987   _____

1986   _____

1985   _____

1984   _____

1983   _____

1982   _____

1981   _____

1980   _____

NOTE: For a complete report on any no-load mutual fund, send your name, address, phone and the name of your fund along with $10 to: J. Stanley Levitt, Inc. 5204 W. 121 Street, Overland Park, KS 66209.

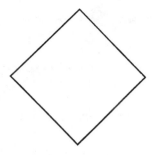

Appendix III: Description of Terms/Abbreviations

NAV:
The *Net Asset Value* or traded price of the mutual fund.

RISK:
For ease of interpretation, the mutual fund's total risk, measured by the fund's standard deviation, has been grouped into five levels:

VHigh	Very High
High	High
AVG	Average
Low	Low
VLow	Very Low

The higher the risk, the higher the expected rate of return. However, database analysis indicates that this is not always the case.

RISK-ADJUSTED PERFORMANCE:
All mutual funds with at least two years of history have been rated and ranked according to two methods of portfolio performance measures. They are the Sharpe and Treynor measures.

SHARPE INDEX:
Also called the Reward-to-Variability measure, is reported by *Money* magazine in its annual mutual fund ratings and is used to measure portfolio performance.   You should rank the performance of your fund based on the Sharpe's index of portfolio performance. A fund return ranking of .6 will be superior to one having a return index of .3.

TREYNOR INDEX:
Also called the Reward-to-Volatility measure, is also used to measure portfolio performance.   Treynor Index is calculated by dividing the same weekly excess return as Sharpe (the risk premium) by the beta coefficient of the fund. Beta is a measure of systematic risk.

Given their similarity, it is usually desirable to measure both indices when evaluating portfolios. The choice between the two being a question of what the investor assumes the risk to be.

Differences in ranking between the two indices result from a lack of complete diversification in the portfolio. Select the funds that rank the highest. The fund's rating has been graded according to the following system:

A+	Outstanding
A-	Excellent
B+	Very Good
B-	Good
C	Fair
D	Poor
F	Fail

When evaluating funds, always evaluate them in terms of return and risk for the following reasons:

- Average rates of return vary widely over time as the market alternates between bullish and bearish periods.

- There is sometimes no relation between the "prospectus" stated objectives and the actual performance of some mutual funds.

- Risk is not considered.

Alpha:
The alpha statistic measures the difference between actual returns provided by a fund and returns that are predicted using either the S&P index for equities and the Merrill Lynch Corporate Master Bond Index for bonds. A positive value means that the fund out-performed the market, on a risk-adjusted basis. The higher the alpha, the better.

Beta:
The beta statistic is a measure of the relationship between a mutual fund's return and market returns, as defined by the S&P 500. The beta measures the sensitivity, volatility, of risk of a mutual fund compared to that of the market.

Div Idx:
The Diversification Index is another name for systematic risk which is measured by the coefficient of determination (R^2). It measures the percentage of a fund's price variability that is explained by the movements of the S&P 500. It gives some indication of how much faith should be placed in its corresponding beta coefficient. The closer the index is to 100, the more reliable is the beta statistics and the more sensitive will the mutual fund react to market news.

Std Dev:
The standard deviation is another measure of uncertainty or risk. The more a mutual fund's return fluctuates around its expected return, the greater is the investor's uncertainty of achieving the return. To differentiate this risk from beta, this statistic is referred to as "the spread".

Corr:
Applies to equities only. The correlation coefficient indicates how closely the mutual fund correlates ("moves together") with the S&P 500. This index will be helpful to investors who are hedging their portfolios.

EXPENSES

Front Load:
Sales charges deducted from the original investment.

Back Load:
    In addition to or in lieu of front loads, some mutual funds assess a fee when the fund is sold:

    D indicates that the fund will assess a fee based upon the initial purchase. The percentage often declines to zero over a period of a few years.

    R can be used to indicate that the fund will assess a fee based upon the amount sold, regardless of your initial purchase. Again, this fee may decline to zero over time.

    C tells you that the mutual fund is closed to new investors.

12b-1:
Not included. These expenses are part of the total yearly expenses; a more meaningful statistic. (See Yly Exp.)

Yly Exp:
This index is the ratio of net expenses to the fund's total asset during the preceding calendar year. Included are management and custodial fees, printing costs, and 12b-1 fees. Here, the total returns and dividend yields (bonds only) are adjusted by the expense ratio.

PORTFOLIO

Asset $Mil:
The total net asset reported at the end of the prior calendar quarter.

Cash:
The cash percentage held in the fund's portfolio at the end of the prior calendar quarter.

Turn:
The rate at which the fund's total portfolio turns over each year. It is computed on a calendar year basis.

PURCHASES

Purchase Mini:
Minimum amount needed to open an account.

Purchase Subsq:
Subsequent minimum amounts.

Value of $1,000:
The value of $1,000 after being left in the fund for three-, five- and ten-years, assuming that all distributions and dividends are reinvested.

OTHER

Tick:
NASDAQ ticker symbol.

Beg:
The year the mutual fund was incorporated.

St:
The state where the fund was incorporated.

Total Return (%) Latest:
This measures, as required by the SEC, the change in the fund's price plus the reinvestment of all dividend and capital gains distributions at the actual reinvestment price. Adjustments are also made for stock splits and miscellaneous distributions:

     1 Mo   The most recent 1 month
     3 Mos   The most recent 3 months
     6 Mos   The most recent 6 months
     12 Mos The most recent 12 months
     YTD   Year-to-date

Gain / Loss:
Measures the change in total return from the previous period. If the total return from the previous period 9.9% and the current period is 5.5%, the information printed will be -4.4%. Present the Gain/Loss for both the one and twelve-month total returns.

Div. Yield:
All income distributions paid during the last 12 months divided by the fund's price reported at the end of the most recent month.

Total Return (%):
For 10 years or the life of the fund year (1980-1989). The total return measures the continuously compounded total return of the fund, including reinvestment of all distributions into additional shares. This is the geometric rate of return.